heart break recovery kitchen

™

heartbreak recovery kitchen™

recipes and remedies
for mending and moving on

Jeanne Ambrose & Lindsey Ambrose

Photos by: Tom Woolery and Jason Bradwell, IKONIX Studio

Handcrafted Words
Des Moines, Iowa

Heartbreak Recovery Kitchen™: Recipes and Remedies for Mending and Moving On
Copyright © 2010 by Jeanne Ambrose & Lindsey Ambrose
Published by Handcrafted Words LLC, Des Moines, Iowa

Library of Congress Cataloging-in-Publication
Data available.

ISBN-10: 0-6153-7492-1
ISBN-13: 978-0-615-37492-5

Production by FRP.INC
P.O. Box 305142
Nashville, TN 37230
800-358-0560

Design by: Bob Riley and Stacey Willey
Cover design by: Bob Riley, Stacey Willey, and Dana Thompson
Photographs by: Tom Woolery and Jason Bradwell, IKONIX Studio
Copy Editor: Martha Long

Printed in the United States of America
First Edition

To Mom/Grandma, who showed us how love and cooking are deliciously intertwined.

acknowledgments

Despite our best efforts to wallow in solitude when times are tough, it's more agreeable to moan and groan over a glass of wine and a plate of pasta. Better still when friends or family are able to whine and dine together.

Although this book caused us a teensy bit of angst, it also brought us many surprising moments with friends: old, new, near, and far.

We are especially grateful to those who helped us with this project:

Bob Riley, an amazing designer with infinite patience, who was in the trenches with us days, nights, and weekends. His goal was to make us happy. We love that in a man.

Debbie Parenza, who rescued us in the recipe-testing department when our energy flagged. Her palate is impeccable. Her generosity and bubbly spirit kept us going when we were running on empty.

Stacey Willey, the über-talented designer who gave birth to the original design concept with us, and who always responded to pleas for advice.

Tom Woolery, photographer extraordinaire, who stepped in and stepped up when challenged with an eleventh-hour project.

Michelle Medley, an old long-distance friend who became a new—and still long-distance—friend after too many years had lapsed. She convinced us to give fear the cold shoulder and embrace life.

Martha Long, our amazingly fast, thorough, and kind copy editor who tried not to look suspicious when we met to exchange layouts and pages in the parking lot of the State Highway Patrol in the dark of night. (It was the halfway point between our homes.)

Elisabeth Ballstadt, whose enthusiasm and positivity is inspiring.

Dana Thompson, the designer who dropped everything to help us design our book cover.

And others who offered their talents and/or kindness along the way: *Robbie Adelman, the team at Applied Art and Technology, Monica Bhide, Jason Bradwell, Sheena Chihak, Beth Damm, Sandra Gerdes, Juli Hale, Lolo Jones, Paul Meesey, Charles Memminger, Sue Mitchell, Rachel Olsson, Renee Schettler Rossi, Sasha Spencer, Susan Strelecki, Kay Stubblefield, Deborah Wagman, and Sandra Wolfe.*

introduction

Everyone's had a reason to throw a bummer bash, even if it's just for a party of one. For instance:

A bad date.

A job layoff.

A vacation that was anything BUT.

A surprise visit by your mother when you were, um, indisposed.

A disparaging email accidentally sent to the person you were dissing.

A breakup or divorce.

Or worse.

You get the picture.

Between the two of us we've experienced plenty of traumatic incidents, from the trivial to the tragic. The trick is knowing how to recover ... or at least move on while you figure out Plan B.

On the other hand, there are days when a girl's just got to wallow in misery and throw her own pity party. And there's nothing wrong with crawling into bed with a bowl of chocolate chip cookie dough*, a spoon, and your remote control.

This book will provide you with recipes that comfort, cheer, or boost your mood. Use them to host a gathering of your most supportive friends or to enjoy solo. There are a few happy distractions smattered throughout the pages, including a list of reasons why you really should indulge in chocolate.

But these dishes are an excuse to step into the kitchen and cook up a bit of happiness. Better to share the final results—and your woes—with others and note the satisfied mood as the food is served up.

As this book goes to press both Lindsey and Jeanne have suffered some pretty major heartbreaks. Jeanne was laid off in what Lindsey dubbed The Great Journalism Purge. She also broke up with a man who brought her gifts in great quantity due to his membership in a big-box store: giant containers of anti-bacterial soap and plastic wrap, for instance.

Lindsey also suffered a breakup with a lover-turned-stalker, flunked a semester's worth of classes, lost her cat and her cell phone (twice), and basically had a long struggle with Murphy and his damnable Law.

Nonetheless, we were always able to mend and move on using food and cooking as therapy.

Want to read more real-life tragedies and mood-mending recipes (both our own and yours)? Check out our website, *heartbreakrecoverykitchen.com*

*Except you shouldn't be eating raw cookie dough because of the raw egg issue. Don't say we didn't warn you.

table of contents

happily ever now

She dreamed.

She wondered.

She imagined the possibilities.

She mulled and contemplated and searched for wisdom.

And then she began.

She began.

And began.

And began again,

Until she figured it out…

And made her own dreams come true.

—Jeanne Ambrose

chapter 1

pity party

Belting out your favorite song relieves angst
like nobody's business. Invite friends to your
bummer bash, bust out the appetizers,
and fire up the karaoke machine.
Croon to your heart's content.

prosciutto roll-ups

Makes 8 appetizer servings.

2 ounces thinly sliced prosciutto

2 ounces herbed bocconcini or feta cheese, cut
into 1×¼-inch pieces *(or thereabouts)*

Fresh chives, cut into 1-inch pieces
(give or take)

Fresh sage or basil leaves *(large leaves*
cut in half)

Olive oil

Finely shredded lemon peel

1. Cut prosciutto slices into strips *(about 2 inches wide)*. Top each prosciutto strip with a piece of cheese. Add 1 or 2 pieces of chives and 1 sage or basil leaf. Roll up.

2. Arrange on a platter. Drizzle with olive oil. Use a Microplane grater to add a shower of lemon peel on top.

WHO NEEDS PILLS?
Listening to a half hour of classical music has the same stress-soothing effect as 10 milligrams of Valium.

candied bacon and chèvre bites

Makes 32 appetizer servings.

2 tablespoons coarsely chopped pecans

2 tablespoons packed brown sugar

½ teaspoon dry mustard

8 slices thick-cut bacon

4 ounces semisoft goat cheese (chèvre)*

1 teaspoon chopped fresh thyme or sage
   (if you want)

1 10- to 12-inch round focaccia, cut into
   32 bite-size pieces

1. Preheat oven to 375°F. Put the nuts in a food processor and whirl until very finely chopped *(or just chop away with a knife on a cutting board).* You want the pieces to be pretty darn small without turning them into nut butter.

2. Toss nuts with brown sugar and dry mustard. Place bacon in a shallow baking pan; press nut mixture on top of bacon. Bake in a 375°F oven for 20-25 minutes or until the bacon is crisp and browned. Peek every once in a while, rotating the pan, if needed, to get the bacon to cook evenly. Remove from oven and place bacon on a paper towel or cookie rack to crisp up. When cool enough to handle, cut each slice into 4 pieces.

3. Meanwhile *(back at the ranch),* combine goat cheese and herbs *(or don't—this is tasty with or without the herbs).* Spread goat cheese on the focaccia bites, and top each with a piece of bacon.

* You can use Cambozola or another creamy blue cheese instead of the chèvre.

blast o' garlic shrimp

Makes 6 to 8 appetizer servings.

2 tablespoons olive oil

1 teaspoon finely shredded lemon peel

2 tablespoons lemon juice

2 cloves garlic, minced

1½ pounds fresh or frozen medium shrimp,
peeled and deveined *(but leave the tails on*
so they're easier to pick up)

2 tablespoons butter

6 cloves garlic, minced

½ teaspoon crushed red pepper

¼ teaspoon sea salt

⅛ to ¼ teaspoon cayenne pepper, if desired
(come on, we dare ya)

1. Make the dipping sauce so it's ready to serve when the shrimp is ready: In a small bowl combine olive oil, lemon peel, lemon juice, and 2 cloves garlic. Done.

2. Thaw shrimp, if frozen. In a big ol' skillet melt butter. Add 6 cloves garlic, stirring vigorously until you can smell the garlic big-time. Add the shrimp to the pan along with the crushed red pepper, salt, and cayenne pepper. Cook and stir until shrimp turns pretty in pink *(opaque)* about 6 minutes. Serve immediately with the dipping sauce.

cheesy artichoke, spinach, and prosciutto bruschetta

Makes 12 to 16 appetizer servings.

1 10-inch round focaccia bread, split in half horizontally so you have a top half and a bottom half *(a serrated knife works best)*

1 tablespoon olive oil

6 slices prosciutto*

1/2 a small sweet onion, chopped *(about ½ cup)*

1 tablespoon butter or olive oil

1 cup shredded Muenster or Havarti cheese

1 cup shredded pepper Jack cheese

1 6-ounce jar marinated artichoke hearts, drained and chopped

1 6-ounce bag fresh baby spinach

1. Preheat oven to 400°F. Place both halves of focaccia bread on a large baking sheet with cut side up. Brush cut sides of bread with olive oil. Bake for 5 minutes or until focaccia is crispy on edges and hot.

2. Meanwhile, in a large skillet heat the prosciutto slices over medium heat until crispy; set aside.

3. In the same skillet cook onion in hot butter over medium heat for 3 to 5 minutes or until soft. Add Muenster, pepper Jack, artichoke hearts, and 4 slices of the prosciutto, crumbled. Cook and stir constantly about 3 minutes or until cheese is melted. Remove from heat and add spinach, stirring until all is well combined.

4. Spread warm cheese mixture on toasted focaccia. Crumble remaining 2 slices of prosciutto over the top. Return to oven and bake for 5 more minutes. Cut into wedges.

*Bacon can be substituted for the prosciutto. Cook bacon in the skillet until crispy. Discard oil and wipe out skillet with a paper towel before adding remaining ingredients.

chicken and mango cucumber bites

Makes about 8 servings.

**3 boneless, skinless chicken breasts
   (about 1 pound)**
**½ of a small apple, cut in matchstick-
   sized strips**
1 medium shallot, minced
⅓ cup mayonnaise
½ of a lime, juiced (about 1 tablespoon)
1 tablespoon olive oil
1 tablespoon curry powder
1 clove garlic, minced
2 medium cucumbers
1 medium mango, finely chopped

1. In a large skillet, cover chicken breasts with water. Bring to boiling; reduce heat. Simmer, covered, for 12 to 14 minutes or the chicken isn't pink in the middle *(an instant read thermometer should read 180°F)*. Drain the water. When the chicken has cooled off enough for you to get your hands on it, shred or chop it.

2. In a medium bowl stir together chicken, apple, mayonnaise, shallot, lime juice, olive oil, curry powder, and garlic.

3. Cut the cucumbers in 2-inch lengths and use a melon baller or a small spoon to scoop out the center most of the way through each section, so you have shells to fill. Spoon the chicken salad into cucumbers until they're heaping full. Top with strips of mango.

orgasmic chorizo-stuffed mushrooms

Makes about 12 appetizer servings.

**8 ounces baby bella mushrooms, cleaned
   and stemmed**

4 ounces chorizo

¼ cup finely chopped onion

4 ounces goat cheese, crumbled

**¼ cup panko bread crumbs or fine dry bread
   crumbs** *(plus a bit for sprinkling on top)*

Salt and pepper

½ cup balsamic vinegar

1 tablespoon honey

1. Preheat oven to 375°F. Place mushrooms, stem side up, on a baking sheet.

2. Cook chorizo and onion in a skillet until the sausage is brown. Don't forget to stir. Drain and blot excess grease with a paper towel. Let sausage cool slightly. Stir goat cheese and panko into the chorizo mixture. Sprinkle with salt and pepper.

3. Top mushroom caps with chorizo mixture. Fill the caps bountifully because the filling shrinks as it bakes. Sprinkle additional panko crumbs on top. Bake for 12 to 15 minutes or until mushrooms are heated through.

4. Meanwhile, combine balsamic vinegar and honey in a small saucepan and simmer until it gets thick and syrupy, about 5 to 10 minutes.

5. Put stuffed 'shrooms on a pretty platter and drizzle with balsamic syrup.

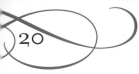

golden caramel corn

Makes about 10 to 11 cups
(about 10 servings).

½ **cup popcorn kernels** *(8 to 9 cups popped)*

2 **cups nuts, such as cashews, slivered almonds,**
   or peanuts

½ **cup unsalted butter**

⅓ **cup light corn syrup**

1 **cup granulated sugar**

¼ **cup brown sugar**

½ **teaspoon vanilla extract**

¼ **teaspoon baking soda**

1. Preheat oven to 250°F. Butter a large roasting pan or a couple of rimmed baking sheets. Toss popped corn and nuts together and spread in roasting pan. Put pan in oven while you make caramel mixture.

2. In a heavy large saucepan, combine butter, corn syrup, and sugar. Cook and stir over medium-high heat until mixture boils. Reduce heat to medium and let it continue to boil gently, stirring frequently, about 10 minutes or until it turns golden brown. A candy thermometer should register 212°F. *(Keep a close eye on it because it can go from perfect caramel color to burnt brown while your back is turned.)*

3. Remove from heat; stir in vanilla. Carefully stir in baking soda but be prepared for a reaction: The mixture will bubble crazily and expand. *(That's why you need a large saucepan.)* Carefully pour caramel mixture over popcorn and nuts; toss gently to coat. Bake caramel-coated popcorn and nuts for 1 hour, stirring every 10 or 15 minutes. Cool slightly and break into clusters. Store in a tightly covered container for up to a week.

easy edamame spread

Makes 1½ cups or so.

**1 10-ounce package shelled edamame,
cooked according to package directions
(save 3 to 4 tablespoons cooking water)**
¼ cup cilantro and/or parsley
2 small shallots
1 clove garlic
½ of a jalapeño pepper, seeds removed
3 tablespoons olive oil
1 tablespoon sesame oil
Juice of 2 limes (about 3 to 4 tablespoons)
1 teaspoon soy sauce
**Vegetables for dipping (sliced cucumbers,
sweet pepper strips, blanched green beans)**

1. Put everything, except veggies for dipping, in the bowl of a food processor. Give it a whirl until smooth.

2. Serve with vegetables. Actually, anything is good with this: chunks of crusty bread, crackers, or your finger if no one's looking.

revenge is a song best played loud

Man done you wrong? Or your boss? Best friend? Simply feeling sorry for yourself? Plenty of powerful singers know just how you feel. Spin these to-hell-with-him/her/it hits, or go for the uplifting, mushy music and wail along.

• **Ace of Base, *The Sign***
("I saw the sign and it opened up my eyes...")

• **Pat Benatar, *Love Is a Battlefield***
("...heartache to heartache we stand...")

• **Beyonce, *Irreplaceable***
("...the truth of the matter is replacing you is so easy.")

• **Kelly Clarkson, *Since U Been Gone***
("...I can breathe for the first time...")

• **The Cyrkle, *Red Rubber Ball***
("And I think it's gonna be all right, yeah, the worst is over now...")

• **Gloria Gaynor, *I Will Survive***
("...you're not welcome anymore.")

• **Buddy Guy, *Damn Right, I've Got the Blues***
("You damn right, I've got the blues..."

• **Israel "Iz" Kamakakiwo'ole, *Somewhere Over the Rainbow***
(Dreams really do come true...")

• **Ingrid Michaelson, *Everybody***
("...swing open up your chest and let it in. Just let the love, love, love begin")

• **The Proclaimers, *I'm On My Way***
("I'm on my way, from misery to happiness today...")

• **Quarterflash, *Harden My Heart***
("...gonna swallow my tears.")

• **Warren Zevon, *Accidentally Like a Martyr***
("Why'd I let you get to me again...)

deep blue funk cocktail
(Adapted with permission from Domaine de Canton)

Makes 1 serving.

1 ounce coconut rum *(Malibu)*

1 ounce light rum

1 ounce ginger liqueur *(Domaine de Canton)*

1 ounce pineapple juice

½ ounce blue curaçao

A squirt of fresh lime juice

1. Fill cocktail shaker with ice. Add all ingredients. Shake. Shake. Shake.

2. Pour into a tall, elegant glass. ***Why not?***

**CRANK UP
THE MUSIC**
Best music to lift your mood? Any kind, say Penn State researchers. From rock/pop to new age, study subjects felt better after listening to whatever music they liked best.

Charles Memminger, Kaneohe, Hawaii

the chain-smoking angel in chef's attire

The summer my mom died I was a college kid cooking in the biggest resort on the Oregon Coast, Salishan Lodge & Golf Resort. I had worked my way up from busboy to fish cook in one of three dining rooms.

Benny ran the mesquite fire grill, and I cooked the salmon, oysters, and Dungeness crab in a cooking line open to the dining room. I was the lowest cook in the resort, but I was a cook. And at Salishan, the cooks were rock stars. And the head chef was God. His second in command, a sous chef with a huge belly and a perpetual cigarette dangling from his lips, was the wrath of God. We feared him. Yet we were still rock stars.

It was a great summer. I surfed the icy waves during the day, cooked at night, and partied after work with the waitresses. There was one bothersome issue: My mother, home in Corvallis, had cancer. I knew she was sick, but I didn't know how sick.

One afternoon as I was cutting salmon fillets, the sous chef with the cigarette walked up to me. He had never spoken to me before, but that day he pushed me back against the cutting board with his belly, leaned his face close to mine, and said, "Be strong for your family. People will need you. You can grieve later." Then he turned and walked away.

A few days later I was in the hospital with my mother, holding her hand as she died. I was destroyed. But I remembered what the sous chef had told me and bucked up for the agonizing next few days and through the funeral.

I returned to Salishan and found comfort in the pressure of the cooking line, baking the salmon, frying the breaded oysters, and sautéing lobster and scallops. I would grieve later. At the end of the summer when our dining room closed, the sous chef summoned me to work on the cooking line for the gourmet dining room. It was the Holy Grail for cooks. I think it was his way of saying, "Cook, son, and everything else will take care of itself."

It wasn't until months later when I finally grieved for my mother. I was on a deserted beach at night, after a day of solo surfing. I remember thinking about unlikely angels. And I realized that one of my angels has a big gut, smokes cigarettes, and wears a chef's uniform.

Charles Memminger is an author and screenwriter in Hawaii.

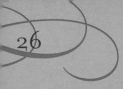

chapter 2

the morning after

So, you and Capt. Morgan engaged in
a sorrow-drowning affair.
Not the best heart-healing approach perhaps,
but there are ways to settle the sloshing and muffle
the throbbing.

huevos divorciados

Makes 2 servings.

Red Salsa *(next page)*

Green Salsa *(next page)*

6 to 7 ounces chorizo *(or ½ cup black beans)*

4 eggs

**4 corn tortillas, toasted in the oven or fried
    until crispy**

Fresh chopped cilantro

Lime wedges

1. Make salsas. Set aside. Crumble and cook chorizo until it turns very dark brown. Drain and blot excess grease with a paper towel. *(It gives up a LOT of grease that you can drain as it cooks, but you still need to blot it with paper towels.)*

2. Cook eggs. Choose sunny-side up, over easy, or whatever way you like them. Then get out 2 plates and start building. For each serving put 2 warm tortillas on a plate, overlapping if needed. Top each tortilla with an egg. Separate eggs with half of the chorizo. Top one egg with Red Salsa and the other with Green Salsa. Sprinkle cilantro over top and squirt on a bit of lime, if you like it.

Two eggs with different personalities (one topped with red salsa, one with green) are separated by chorizo in this huevos divorciados, or divorced eggs, dish. Refried beans, black beans, or a dollop of guacamole can be used in place of the chorizo.

green salsa (*salsa verde*)

4 small tomatillos, finely chopped
   (*peel off the papery husks first*)
1 small avocado, peeled, pitted, and chopped
¼ cup finely chopped shallot or onion
1 clove garlic, minced
½ of a small poblano pepper, seeded and
   finely chopped
½ cup crumbled fresh cotija cheese
   (*feta cheese is a good substitute, but this is
   a Mexican recipe*)

1. Skip all the chopping and mincing and just toss everything—except the avocado and cheese—in a food processor and set it awhirl until salsa is nearly smooth. Stir in avocado and cheese.

red salsa (*salsa roja*)

1 large tomato, chopped (*about 1¼ cups*)
¼ cup finely chopped shallot or onion
1 clove garlic, minced
½ small poblano pepper, seeded and finely
   chopped (*or jalapeño*)
1 tablespoon chopped fresh cilantro
   (*Lindsey skips the cilantro*)
1 teaspoon lime juice
Salt (*a couple of shakes*)

1. Mix everything together. Or use the food processor as directed in the Green Salsa recipe, at left.

There's plenty of salsa here. Cover and refrigerate the extra for a day or two. Slather some on a burger in place of ketchup.

the two-minute omelet (give or take)

Makes 1 hefty serving *(or 2 small portions, which is about the size we should be eating anyway).*

1 tablespoon butter

2 eggs

2 tablespoons water

Dash of salt and pepper

½ cup filling*

1. In an 8- to 10-inch nonstick skillet melt butter over medium-high heat until just hot enough to sizzle when a drop of water is added. Meanwhile, whisk together eggs, water, salt, and pepper. Pour eggs into hot skillet.

2. As eggs set, use a spatula to carefully push cooked portions at edges toward center of skillet, lifting eggs so the uncooked portions flow underneath.

3. When eggs are just set, gently sprinkle filling on half of omelet. Fold omelet in half over filling. Slide omelet onto plate. *Et voila.*

*Fillings for omelets are limitless. For instance:
- Feta cheese and chopped kalamata olives
- Chopped avocado, salsa, and sour cream
- Sautéed onions and mushrooms
- Steamed asparagus, snipped herbs, and chives

lemon ricotta pancakes with strawberry sauce

Makes 4 servings
(about eight 3- to 4-inch pancakes)

Fresh Strawberry Sauce (recipe below, right)

½ **cup flour**

2 **tablespoons sugar**

2 **teaspoons baking powder**

¼ **teaspoon salt**

1 **cup ricotta cheese (you can use nonfat ricotta, but you'll be sorry)**

2 **eggs, beaten**

¼ **cup milk**

1 **tablespoon finely shredded lemon peel (this adds a fresh "oh, yes" to these pancakes, but it's OK to leave out. Instead add 1 teaspoon of vanilla and maybe even a sprinkling of cinnamon)**

1. In a bowl combine flour, sugar, baking powder, and salt. Whisk in ricotta, eggs, milk, and lemon peel. Whisk until smooth, adding a smidge more milk if you like. But this batter should be more thick than thin.

3. For each pancake, pour or ladle a little less than ¼ cup batter onto a hot, lightly oiled skillet. Gently spread into a 3- to 4-inch circle. *(You don't want a real thick pancake, do you?)* Cook over medium heat about 2 minutes or until top starts to bubble and bottom is golden brown. Flip pancakes; cook another 1 to 2 minutes. Serve with Fresh Strawberry Sauce.

Fresh Strawberry Sauce: Gently mash 1 cup fresh strawberries with 1 teaspoon sugar. Let sit at room temperature for 10 minutes. Stir.

fried rice with portuguese sausage

Makes 4 hearty servings.

2 tablespoons oil *(divided)*

1 small onion, chopped

1 carrot, chopped

**1 large jalapeño pepper, seeds and veins
removed, and finely chopped** *(or if you don't
want it spicy, substitute ½ of a sweet
pepper, chopped)*

3 cloves garlic, minced

**12 ounces Portuguese sausage linguiça,
Andouille, or Polish sausage, sliced**

3 cups leftover cooked rice

2 teaspoons hoisin sauce

1 tablespoon soy sauce or fish sauce

4 green onions, sliced

1. Heat 1 tablespoon of the oil over medium-high heat in a wok or deep skillet. Add onion, carrot, and jalapeño pepper. Cook and stir for 3 to 4 minutes or until onion begins to soften. Add garlic, stirring for about 30 seconds. Add sausage slices; cook and stir for 3 minutes more.

2. If needed, add remaining oil. Stir in rice, hoisin, and soy sauce. Cook and stir for 1 to 2 minutes more or until rice is heated through. Sprinkle with green onions.

fully loaded home-fried potatoes

Makes 2 hungry-person servings.

¼ cup chopped onion

1 red sweet pepper, chopped
   (you do know you can use any color pepper, don't you? red is prettier, and green tastes so darn, well, green)

2 cloves garlic, minced

4 tablespoons butter and/or olive oil

1 teaspoon ground ginger *(or 2 teaspoons grated fresh ginger)*

¼ teaspoon smoked hot paprika or paprika

2 large leftover baked potatoes or 1 Russet and 1 sweet potato, peels on or off *(or cooked in the microwave oven)*, **about 1½ pounds**

½ teaspoon salt

Freshly ground black pepper
   (2 to 6 cranks, depending on how peppery you're feeling)

1. Cook onion, red pepper, and garlic in hot butter over medium heat for about 5 minutes or until onion is tender. Stir in ginger and paprika. Cut potatoes into bite-size cubes. Add to skillet, stirring to combine. Sprinkle with salt and pepper.

2. Cook without stirring for 7 to 8 minutes or until a golden-brown crust forms on the bottom of potatoes. Flip potatoes. Cook for 2 to 3 minutes more, stirring occasionally, until heated through.

hangover helpers

Lots of old wives' tales offer hangover remedies, some more reputable than others. But why not give 'em a try? Here's our short list.

Part of the reason you feel as if your head is stuffed with fluff after a night of extreme imbibing is that you're dehydrated. There are other factors involved, but who cares about science at a time like this?

You already know not to drink alcohol on an empty stomach, right? Right? Food in your stomach slows the absorption of alcohol into your system.

- **Gobbling greasy food** on the morning after may be a fabled cure, but it works for us. Carbs seem to soak up a lot of whatever's sloshing around in your stomach, too.

- **Pop a couple of pain relievers** followed by a chaser of ginger tea or water and crawl back into bed until the guy with the sledgehammer leaves your brain.

- **Hydrate. Hydrate. Hydrate.** We're not talking about drinking more alcohol, which is a diuretic. We're talking water, hold the Scotch. Just hoist one tall glass of water for every adult beverage you consume.

- **Steer clear of shots,** dark liquors, and too many froufrou drinks. And stick to one type of poison. Don't pound tequila, chug a beer to chase, and then finish with a rum and coke!

- **Choose white over red wine,** vodka instead of Scotch, whiskey, or dark rum. And light beer is not quite as buzz-inducing as the heavy stuff.

ginger cucumber water

Makes eight 8-ounce servings.

2 cups boiling water

1-inch piece peeled fresh ginger, cut in thin slices

6 cups chilled water

½ of a small cucumber, sliced

4 sprigs pineapple sage, slightly crushed

*(use whatever herbs sound good to you, or skip
'em because the ginger-cucumber combo is a
pretty dynamic duo on its own)*

1. Pour boiling water over ginger. Let steep for
5 minutes. Remove ginger slices. *(Or if you put the
ginger slices in a tea ball you won't have to worry
about plucking the ginger out of the hot water.)*
Cool the ginger water.

2. Combine ginger water with remaining
ingredients. Chill at least one hour. Serve over ice.
If you fish out the cucumber slices after
4 to 6 hours, the water will keep for 3 days.

orange herb water

Makes eight 8-ounce servings.

1 orange

½ of a lemon, thinly sliced

4 sprigs cinnamon basil, slightly crushed

   (or use lemon basil, mint, or rosemary)

½ gallon chilled water

1. Remove large strips of orange peel from half of the orange, being careful not to cut into the white pith *(it can be bitter)*. Cut remaining half of orange into thin slices.

2. Combine orange peel, orange slices, lemon slices, and cinnamon basil with water in a pitcher. Chill at least one hour. Serve over ice. Store in refrigerator up to 3 days.

key lime mint water

Makes eight 8-ounce servings.

½ gallon chilled water

4 key limes, thinly sliced

4 sprigs fresh mint, slightly crushed

1. Combine ingredients in a pitcher and chill for about an hour. Serve over ice. Will keep in the refrigerator for up to 3 days. The lime flavor gets stronger the longer it stays in the water.

bloody mary with bacon

Makes 2 servings.

2 lime wedges

Bacon Salt *(baconsalt.com)* or coarse salt

1½ cups tomato juice

1 tablespoon lime juice

1 teaspoon Worcestershire sauce

1 teaspoon dill pickle juice or olive brine

¼ teaspoon horseradish or hot sauce to taste
    (some like it hot)

Freshly ground pepper

2 to 3 ounces of vodka *(or skip if you
    don't believe in that hair-of the-dog thing)*

2 crispy-cooked bacon strips

1. Rub lime wedge around rim of 2 glasses. Dip rims in Bacon Salt. Combine remaining ingredients, except bacon strips, in a large cocktail mixer and shake. *(Or put ingredients in a small pitcher and stir.)* Pour Bloody Mary into 2 ice-filled glasses. Lay one bacon strip across the top of each glass, or crumble on top.

Make a meal out of your Bloody Mary. Add fully loaded swizzle sticks using shrimp, cherry tomatoes, chunks of cheese, or a small smoked fish. In the fishing town of Leland, Michigan, they tuck a smoked chub, tail first, into each drink and call it a Chubby Mary.

chapter 3

when life hands you lemons

Sometimes a girl's got to suck up the sour
and focus on the zest.
Or take that lemon and make it
your main squeeze.
And pucker up, baby.

easy lemon-garlic chicken

Makes 6 servings.

Olive oil

3½ pounds chicken thighs or breasts

2 lemons, sliced

¾ cup kalamata olives, pitted

6 cloves garlic, peeled

½ cup dry white wine *(chicken broth if you're not imbibing)*

1 teaspoon sea salt

½ teaspoon crushed red pepper flakes

1. Preheat oven to 375°F. Drizzle a smidge of olive oil in a roasting pan *(13x9 will do)*. Add chicken, lemon, olives, garlic, and wine. Drizzle a little more olive oil over chicken. Sprinkle with sea salt and red pepper flakes.

2. Roast for 35 to 45 minutes. It's done when chicken reaches 180°F. Use an instant-read thermometer, but don't let it touch bone.

The secret to big, juicy flavor is bone-in, skin-on chicken. Remove the skin after chicken is cooked, if you insist. We're not responsible for the dry results if you use skinless, boneless chicken breasts.

lemon chicken lasagna

Makes 4 to 6 servings, depending on everyone's appetite.

Cooking spray

¼ cup butter

2 cloves garlic, squished through a garlic press

¼ cup flour

3 cups milk

2 tablespoons drained capers

2 teaspoons finely shredded lemon peel, divided *(use a fine grater and make sure you don't get any of the white pith)*

6 lasagna noodles *(give or take; you may have to cut off a couple inches of the cooked noodles to fit in the square pan)*

1 cup ricotta cheese *(cottage cheese is an OK substitute if you're not a food snob)*

1¾ cups shredded cheese *(we like to mix it up: mozzarella, a bit of extra-sharp cheddar, and/or some crumbled feta cheese, and maybe a smidge of Parmesan)*

12 ounces cooked chicken breast, cut into edible chunks

1. Preheat oven to 350°F. Lightly coat an 8×8-inch or 9×9-inch baking pan with cooking spray; set aside. Melt butter in a saucepan. Add garlic and cook over low heat for 1 minute. Stir in flour, cooking until mixture is thick and golden brown. Increase heat to medium and add milk; cook and stir until thick and bubbly. Stir in capers and 1 teaspoon of the lemon peel.

2. Cook lasagna according to package directions; drain. Spoon ⅓ cup of sauce into baking pan. Top with 3 noodles. Spoon ½ cup of the ricotta cheese and ½ cup of the shredded cheese over noodles. Top with half of the chicken. Spoon half of the remaining sauce over chicken layer.

3. Top with 3 more noodles, remaining ricotta, another ½ cup shredded cheese, and remaining chicken. Add 3 more noodles, remaining sauce, and remaining cheese.

4. Cover with foil. Bake for 40 minutes. Remove from oven and let stand, covered, for 15 to 20 minutes. To serve, uncover and sprinkle with remaining 1 teaspoon lemon peel.

very lemon pasta with spinach

Makes 4 servings.

8 ounces penne pasta *(or whatever you've got in the pantry)*

4 tablespoons butter

½ cup half-and-half or milk *(cream if you don't care about the calories or the artery-clogging issue)*

2 teaspoons finely shredded lemon peel *(use a Microplane grater to shred peel before cutting the lemon to squeeze out juice)*

3 tablespoons fresh lemon juice

3 tablespoons capers, drained

2 cups baby spinach *(or sliced summer squash or zucchini, whatever strikes your fancy)*

Salt and freshly ground black pepper

Fresh grated Parmesan cheese *(or feta, mmmm, feta)*

1. Cook pasta according to package directions; drain, reserving ½ cup of the pasta water.

2. While pasta is cooking, melt butter in a large, deep skillet over medium heat. Stir in half-and-half and lemon juice.

3. Add the pasta to the skillet with the lemon peel, capers, and ⅓ cup of the pasta water; toss. *(Add more pasta cooking liquid 1 tablespoon at a time, if necessary.)* Toss in spinach; add salt and pepper to taste. Serve with cheese.

Make this a one-dish wonder by tossing finished pasta with 1 pound of cooked shrimp, peeled and deveined, of course.

lemony chickpea and herb salad

Makes 4 servings.

**1 15-ounce can garbanzo beans (chickpeas),
   rinsed and drained**
**¼ cup chopped fresh herbs (we like mint,
   parsley, basil, and/or oregano)**
**1 tablespoon finely chopped green onions
   or chives**
1 teaspoon finely shredded lemon peel
2 tablespoons lemon juice
1 tablespoon olive oil
½ of a sweet pepper, chopped (about ⅔ cup)
1 small roma tomato, chopped (½ cup)
1 small cucumber, chopped (about 1 cup)
½ cup feta cheese
Salt and pepper

1. Toss together the garbanzo beans, herbs, green onions, lemon peel, lemon juice, and olive oil. Mash the chickpea mixture with a fork until everything is smooshed together but still a little chunky. Stir in sweet pepper, tomato, cucumber, feta cheese, salt, and pepper. Done.

Pile this pleasingly puckery combo on half a ciabatta roll and call it lunch. Or serve it as a side salad.

roasted asparagus and carrots with lemon oil

Makes 4 to 6 servings.

⅓ cup olive oil

1 large lemon, thinly sliced

¼ cup fresh sage leaves

1 pound fresh asparagus, trimmed

8 ounces baby carrots, halved the long way
   (or medium carrots, peeled and cut into
   sticks about the size of french fries)

Coarse sea salt or salt

1. Preheat oven to 450°F. In a skillet heat olive oil over medium heat. Add lemon slices. Cook about 4 minutes or until lemons begin to brown. Flip slices over. Add sage to the oil. Cook about 1 minute more *(or less)* until sage gets crispy. Remove the lemon slices* and sage; set aside. Save the lemony oil *(you should have about ¼ cup)*.

2. Put asparagus and carrots in a baking pan or roasting pan. Drizzle with the lemony oil. Sprinkle with salt. Toss to combine. Spread vegetables out in the pan. Roast for 10 to 15 minutes or until crisp-tender, stirring a few times during roasting. To serve, add cooked lemon slices and sage to vegetables; gently toss.

*At this point, Lindsey chops up the succulent cooked fruit to mix with the roasted vegetables (tossing the lemon rind in the compost bin).

so long, stress

Heartbreak ratchets up the stress factor. But there are simple, right-now ways to turn the stress down. Chill out by taking a few tips from experts.

- **Picture something positive in your mind—** your ideal vacation spot, a chocolate orgy, an especially aesthetic posterior—and keep it there for at least 30 seconds.

- **Reach for a tube of Rubylicious Red lipstick.** During periods of strain (including job loss, endless gray skies, or the crashing of your hard drive), you still want to feel good. Little treats—like a fun lipstick—are proven pick-me-ups.

- **Pull out the photo album** (the digital version or the old-fashioned kind) and let the reminiscing begin. Researchers from Loyola University say reliving happy times for just 20 minutes a day can make you more cheerful.

- **Sniff something soothing.** Inhaling the scent of lemon, mango, lavender, or other aromatic plants may ease stress. Scientists in Japan report that sniffing certain fragrances can alter gene activity and blood chemistry in ways that can take stress levels down a notch.

- **Take a mind trip.** Think of a place and time in your life when you were oh so mellow. Engage all of your senses. Hear the gentle waves, feel the warmth of the sun, and taste the salt of that margarita. Ahhh.

- **Turn your focus to your surroundings.** Really paying attention to the here and now leaves less room for those stressful thoughts.

white wine and citrus butter

Makes ¾ cup.

½ cup dry white wine

¼ cup orange juice *(or water)*

¼ cup lemon juice*

3 tablespoons finely grated lemon peel

1 tablespoon chopped green onions

1 clove garlic, minced

½ cup *(1 stick)* **unsalted butter, cut into
    small pieces**

Fresh lemon-thyme leaves *(or just a hint of
    any mild herb)*

1. In small saucepan combine wine, orange juice, lemon juice, green onions, and garlic. Cook over medium heat, stirring occasionally, until mixture is reduced to about ¼ cup and is almost syrupy. *(Be patient. It takes 15 to 20 minutes.)*

2. Turn heat to low. Stir in lemon peel. Add butter, one piece at a time, whisking until each piece is melted before adding the next piece. *(Watch and whisk constantly. Think low and slow. If the sauce gets too hot, it will curdle.)* Purists like to strain out the tasty tidbits of green onions, garlic, and peel, but we leave 'em in. Sprinkle with fresh herbs just before serving over cooked fish, chicken, eggs, or veggies.

***Remove the yellow zest with a Microplane or fine grater before you squeeze the juice from the lemon. It's easier that way.**

This sauce doesn't reheat well: It likes to curdle. But you can make it, then keep it warm in a thermal coffee mug. (Sniff the mug first. You don't want it to smell like coffee.)

limoncello with a hint of lime

Makes about 4 cups, which translates to about 32 icy cold shots to down. Alternately, you could pour your luscious limoncello over ice cream, shortcake, pound cake, or use it to mix up a cocktail.

12 lemons

1 lime

3½ cups vodka *(go for 95- to 100-proof vodka. We used 150-proof grain alcohol— Everclear—because we live in a state where it's not banned, neener, neener)*

½ cup vanilla vodka *(like Absolut)*

½ cup sugar

½ cup water

1. Use a Microplane or fine grater to finely shred peel of all 13 fruits. In a large jar, combine the shredded peel and the vodka. Seal tightly and place in a cool, dark place for 2 to 4 weeks, depending on your patience.

2. When you can't stand it anymore, pull out the jar. Put it on the counter while you make a simple syrup by combining the sugar and water in a small saucepan. Bring to boil, stirring until sugar dissolves. Let cool.

3. Strain the vodka mixture several times through cotton cheesecloth or coffee filters. Make sure all the lemon peel is gone. Your goal is to have a clear yellow liquid. Add the sugar syrup and stir to combine. Use a funnel to pour limoncello into a bottle and seal with a cork. Place in a cool, dark place for at least 1 week. If you can stand it, let it age for a month or more. Then stash it in the freezer until ready to serve.

Homemade limoncello in Italy often is "aged" for 1 year before it is deemed delicious enough to drink. The flavor is supposed to get smoother the longer it sits. We've never had the patience to wait that long.

easy frozen lemonade margaritas

Makes about 8 servings.

4 cups crushed ice

1 cup frozen lemonade concentrate

½ cup frozen limeade concentrate
    (or 1 cup frozen strawberries)

¾ cup tequila

¼ cup triple sec

Zest of 1 lime *(about 1 tablespoon)*

Lime wedges

Coarse salt

1. Put crushed ice, lemonade concentrate, lime concentrate, tequila, and triple sec in a blender. Cover and blend until slushy.

2. Rub rims of margarita glass with lemon wedge. Dip rim in salt. Fill glass with margaritas. Sprinkle with lime zest.

Yeah, yeah, yeah. We know this isn't for margarita purists, but it's a quick and easy way to serve a crowd. Besides, purists suck down their margaritas on the rocks.

Deborah Wagman, Laporte, Minnesota

debilitation, then discovery

Long ago—when men ruled the workplace and a woman's place was in the kitchen (meaning the kitchen at home)—I became a chef. As a 100-pound female employee in a restaurant filled with brawny males, I had a lot to prove.

I did it by becoming as physically strong as they were.

I could easily hoist a 100-pound bag of flour over my shoulder and carry 10 gallons of water from sink to stove. I became the bench-press queen at the gym. My strength was my greatest asset. I was, proudly, the Arnold Schwarzenegger of female chefs.

But one day I was hit by a train. Not a literal train, though my outcome was no less painful. This train came without warning—no flashing lights, no lowered crossing gates—in the form of rheumatoid arthritis. The disease made the smallest motions of everyday life excruciatingly torturous. Suddenly I was unable to press the toaster lever, much less bench-press 80 pounds.

After many debilitating months—defeated in a pathetic heap of my own misery—I remembered the words of two of the most important women in my life. The first was my favorite English professor, who wrote in my grad school recommendation, "Deborah's writing, at its best, is simply breathtaking." Then came my mother, who reminded me, "Bloom where you're planted."

Their words—the catalysts for my heartbreak recovery—helped meld my past with my future in a career that uses the strength of my mind instead of my body. Today—I am happy to say—I am a successful food writer.

Deborah Wagman is a food writer and editor who lives and works on a peaceful lake in northern Minnesota.

feng shui your heart

Clear out the bad juju
and get the auspicious
chi flowing.
Fusion food and fusion fun
can heal all wounds.

fiery potstickers

Makes 30 potstickers.

8 ounces ground pork or extra-firm tofu

4 ounces chopped mushrooms

1 cup thinly sliced Chinese cabbage or coleslaw mix

½ cup diced carrots

¼ cup chopped green onions

2 cloves garlic, minced

1 tablespoon finely grated fresh ginger

1 tablespoon soy sauce

1 tablespoon sambal chili sauce or hot sauce

1 tablespoon lemon juice

30 potsticker or wonton wrappers

Canola or other cooking oil

1. Stir together all ingredients, except potsticker wrappers and oil, until combined. Spoon 1 heaping teaspoonful onto the center of each wrapper. *(It's closer to 2 teaspoons, but double-dipping takes too long.)* Moisten edges with water. Fold potsticker wrappers over filling to make a half-moon shape *(or triangle if using square wonton wrappers)*. Press edges tightly to seal.

2. Heat 2 tablespoons oil in a large skillet. Add several potstickers. Cook, uncovered, over medium heat for 2 to 3 minutes. Turn heat to low. Carefully add ⅓ cup water *(oil might splatter)*. Cover and cook for 5 to 7 minutes. Uncover and cook for 3 to 5 minutes more or until water evaporates. Use a spatula to loosen potstickers. Cook for 1 minute more or until bottoms are golden brown.

3. Keep warm in a 300°F oven while you repeat step 2 with remaining potstickers, adding only 1 tablespoon of oil.

In Chinese cuisine, potstickers are good luck charms. Nearly every culture has a version: gyoza, ravioli, pierogi, kreplach. So choose your charm.

thai chicken lettuce wraps

Makes 6 appetizer servings
(2 wraps per serving).

¼ cup light soy sauce

2 tablespoons fresh lime juice

2 cloves garlic, minced

2 teaspoons grated fresh ginger

1 teaspoon sambal chili sauce*

4 green onions, chopped *(about 2 tablespoons)*

1 pound boneless, skinless chicken breasts,
   cut in bite-size strips

¼ cup peanut butter

12 Boston or butterhead lettuce leaves

1 cup matchstick carrots

1 large cucumber, peeled and chopped

¼ cup chopped peanuts

Fresh mint and/or cilantro leaves *(a handful)*

1. Combine soy, lime juice, garlic, ginger, sambal, and green onions. Place chicken in a shallow glass bowl. Pour half of the soy mixture over chicken. Cover and refrigerate for 30 minutes to 2 hours.

2. Meanwhile, make peanut sauce by adding peanut butter to remaining half of soy mixture. Heat in microwave or on stovetop until peanut butter softens. Stir to combine. Add 1 to 2 tablespoons water to reach desired consistency. This is your peanut dipping sauce.

3. Cook chicken in hot oil over medium heat for 4 to 5 minutes or until fully cooked.

4. Arrange lettuce, chicken, carrots, cucumber, peanuts, and mint or cilantro leaves on a platter. Pile fillings on lettuce leaf. Drizzle with peanut sauce. Fold lettuce leaf in half or roll like a burrito.

* Sambal is a condiment, not a Latin dance. It's kinda like an extremely spicy ketchup. Find it in Asian markets or use your favorite hot sauce instead.

tom kha gai soup (Thai coconut soup with chicken)

Makes 4 to 6 servings.

1 14-ounce can low-sodium chicken broth

1 14-ounce can coconut milk (use lowfat if you are so inclined), divided

1 cup water

5 cloves garlic, peeled and smashed lightly with knife

2 Thai chile or serrano peppers, veins and seeds removed (cut hot peppers in quarters)

1- inch piece of ginger, peeled and cut into 4 pieces

2 stalks lemongrass*, outer leaves removed (use only bottom white part of stalk)

8 ounces boneless, skinless chicken breast, cut in bite-size strips

8 ounces straw or other mushrooms, sliced if large (omit if skeptical of mushrooms)

1 cup fresh spinach

3 to 4 green onions, sliced

1 tablespoon fish sauce

1 tespoon soy sauce

Lime wedges

Fresh cilantro (optional)

1. In a large soup pot, combine broth, ⅔ of the coconut milk *(save the rest for later)*, water, garlic, chile peppers, ginger, and lemongrass. Bring to boiling. Add chicken. Return to boiling; reduce heat and simmer for 5 to 8 minutes, or until chicken is no longer pink.

2. Add mushrooms. Simmer for 5 minutes more to intensify the flavors. Fish out the lemongrass, and ginger *(if you don't want people eating them)*. Add spinach, green onions, fish sauce, and soy sauce, and remaining coconut milk. Remove from heat. Let the soup sit and stew for a few minutes before serving with lime wedges for squeezing and cilantro for sprinkling on top.

* When lemongrass is not available, substitute ½ teaspoon lemon zest and ¼ teaspoon lime zest .

hedging all bets

Occasionally you have to remind yourself to breathe in, breathe out. Slooooowly.

Whether you seek solace in prayer, meditation, yoga, or a tub full of bubbles with a glass of wine in hand, tranquility works wonders on a shattered soul and may even heal the body.

No matter what your belief system, research confirms the mind-body effect. Meditation reduces blood pressure. Prayer has a soothing impact. Forcing a smile at least twice a day reduces depression. The placebo effect is valid.

Transcend the miniscule irritants in your life whenever possible. And to get into a Zen zone, check out these feng shui tidbits.

• **The burners on your stove represent wealth**, but you've actually got to use them to reap the benefits. Keep on cooking.

• **Power up your romance area** (the right rear section of your home as you face the front door) by making room for love. Free up closet space by donating outgrown or rarely worn clothes. Get rid of your ex's old love letters. Make sure the wall you face while you're in bed contains artwork that makes you swoon.

• **Clutter is a mood killer.** Tidy up. Feel the relief.

• **Enhance your career area** (in the north part of your house or room) by including a water element, whether it is a tabletop fountain, a glass of water, or a picture of the ocean. Water is considered fortuitous for professional development.

• **Dangle a crystal here and there** to provide sparkling energy.

spicy crab salad

Makes about 3 cups.

1 Japanese or hothouse cucumber, cut into matchstick pieces

2 medium carrots, julienned

1 12-ounce package surimi* *(imitation crab)* **sliced into strips roughly the size of the cukes**

⅓ cup mayonnaise

2 teaspoons rice vinegar or lemon juice

2 teaspoons sesame oil

2 teaspoons Sriracha chili sauce

1 teaspoon soy sauce

1 to 2 tablespoons toasted sesame seeds and/or furikake

1 ripe avocado, peeled, pitted, and cut into chunks

1. Place cucumber, carrots, and surimi in a bowl. To make the sauce, stir together mayo, rice vinegar, sesame oil, Sriracha, and soy sauce. Add sauce to surimi mixture and toss gently to combine. Gently mix in avocado. Sprinkle with sesame seeds and/or furikake.

2. Serve immediately as is or atop a bed of greens drizzled with Asian salad dressing. It also makes a perfect topping for sushi.

*You can substitute cooked and flaked real crabmeat for the surimi. Let your budget help you decide.

build your own sushi

Makes 4 to 6 servings *(3 to 4 pieces per serving).*

2 tablespoons rice vinegar

1 tablespoon sugar

¼ teaspoon salt

3 cups cooked short-grain rice

8 sheets of nori *(seaweed)*, each sheet cut
   in half

2 to 3 tablespoons wasabi paste

Variety of sushi toppings, such as cooked
   shrimp, avocado slices, shredded carrots,
   cucumber cut into matchstick pieces, thinly
   sliced spinach, and/or Spicy Crab Salad
   (see recipe, page 56)

Toasted sesame seeds or furikake

Soy sauce

1. In a small glass bowl *(microwave safe)*, combine vinegar, sugar, and salt. Cook in the microwave for 30 seconds; stir until sugar is dissolved. Drizzle vinegar mixture over cooked rice. Stir gently until mixture is absorbed.

2. For each hand-rolled sushi, top one piece of nori with about 1 tablespoon rice, making sure rice is tightly packed and only covers half of the nori sheet. Spread a tiny bit of wasabi paste on rice. Add toppings of your choice. Sprinkle with toasted sesame seeds. Roll into a cone shape. Serve with soy sauce for dipping.

Really. It's not raw fish. Many people believe that sushi always involves raw fish. Not necessarily. It often contains just vegetables and sometimes cooked crab, shrimp, or salmon. In Hawaii, Spam sushi is a top seller.

green curry shrimp and green beans

Makes 4 servings.

2 tablespoons oil

1 medium onion, chopped

1½ cups halved green beans

1 small sweet bell pepper, cut in thin strips

1 14-ounce can unsweetened coconut milk

½ cup chicken broth or water

1 medium zucchini, thinly sliced

3 cloves garlic, minced

3 tablespoons Thai green curry paste

1 tablespoon fish sauce or soy sauce

1 pound shelled, deveined shrimp or skinless, boneless chicken, cut in bite-size pieces

Hot cooked rice or noodles

Fresh Thai basil or basil, chopped coarsely

1. Heat oil over medium heat in a wok or large skillet. Add onion, green beans, and pepper. *(If using chicken instead of shrimp, add chicken now, too.)* Cook and stir for 5 to 8 minutes.

2. Add coconut milk, broth, zucchini, garlic, curry paste, and fish sauce. Bring to boiling; reduce heat and simmer for 8 to 10 minutes. Add shrimp and cook for 2 to 3 minutes more or until shrimp turn pink and opaque. Serve over cooked rice or noodles. Top with basil.

asian shrimp noodles with vegetables

Makes 4 servings.

8 to 12 ounces fresh or frozen peeled, deveined, cooked medium shrimp

2 cups cooked noodles *(3 to 4 ounces, uncooked)*

¼ cup Asian sesame salad dressing or sesame-ginger dressing *(we're partial to Newman's Own brand)*

1 carrot, chopped

½ of a red sweet pepper, cut in thin strips

2 green onions, sliced *(3 tablespoons)*

¼ teaspoon red pepper flakes

1 cup snow peas, blanched*, drained, and cut in half

¼ cup chopped peanuts

2 tablespoons snipped fresh cilantro

1. Thaw shrimp, if frozen; set aside.

2. In a large bowl toss warm pasta with Asian dressing. Add carrot, sweet pepper, onions, and red pepper flakes to pasta. Toss to combine. Cover and refrigerate 1 to 24 hours.

3. Before serving, gently toss in snow peas and shrimp. Add additional Asian dressing, if noodles seem dry. Top with peanuts and cilantro.

*Blanching is an easy technique to keep vegetables crisp and tender. Drop the vegetables briefly into boiling water, drain, then drop them in ice water to chill.

This is a dish with lots of wiggle room. Some noodle options: udon, rice, ramen, or even spaghetti or fettuccine noodles. Swap the shrimp with cooked, chicken, pork, or tofu. You can pretty much clean out the fridge and invent a new dish every day.

change your fortune cookies

Makes about 18 cookies.

¼ cup butter, melted

1 teaspoon grated fresh ginger or ½ teaspoon ground ginger

½ teaspoon vanilla

⅛ teaspoon ground cinnamon

Dash of ground cloves

2 egg whites

½ cup sugar

½ cup all-purpose flour

½ cup bittersweet, dark, or semisweet chocolate, chopped

1 teaspoon shortening

1. Preheat oven to 375° F. Line cookie sheet with a silicone nonstick baking mat, foil, or parchment paper; lightly coat with nonstick cooking spray. Combine butter, ginger, vanilla, cinnamon, and cloves. Set aside.

2. Beat egg whites and sugar with an electric mixer on medium speed for about 1 minute. Add about half of the flour; beat until mixed. Fold in butter mixture. Add remaining flour; beat until combined.

3. Drop 1 tablespoon batter onto cookie sheet, and spread with back of spoon into 3½-inch circles. Bake only 3 to 4 cookies at a time.

4. Bake for 7 to 8 minutes or until cookies begin to brown around the edges. Let cookies cool on cookie sheet for about 30 seconds. Then work quickly to remove cookies, one at a time, from sheet. Place cookie on a dish towel and use towel to fold cookie in half, pinching at top (*we use our bare hands, because we're tough*). Gently bend ends together to form fortune cookie shape. *(Tip: Folding the cookie over a chopstick can help form the bend in the center.)* Place cookies in muffin tin to hold their shape while they cool.

5. Write fortunes on long strips of sturdy paper and thread through cooled cookies.

6. Melt chocolate and shortening in a glass bowl or measuring cup in the microwave. Dip half of cookie in melted chocolate. Sprinkle with chopped peanuts or candied sprinkles.

fortune hunting

Go ahead and have fun when you're writing fortunes to slip inside the cookies. Create personalized messages specific to each cookie recipient. Or use some of these if you want to give your brain a break.

Your body is your temple. Provide offerings of dark chocolate and wine to the mouth altar.

Create a saucy, confident alter-ego. Let HER do the talking.

Seek solace in solitude.

Dance with wild abandon daily.

Just be you, and the rest will follow.

Soon you will have more than enough money to share.

Eat. Drink. Laugh. Love.

Expect the best.

The choice is always yours. Choose the good stuff.

You're blue. Boo hoo. Get over it.

Rachel Olsson, Santa Fe, New Mexico

a rebirth

I was in my final semester of nursing school when I realized that the pharmaceutical/factory system of health care (move 'em in, load 'em up, move 'em out) was not for me. Even though I could push myself through that last semester, there was no way I was going to work as a nurse. The hospital-based program had effectively killed my soul.

That was when I had the opportunity to attend a lecture by Patch Adams, the doctor whose life was portrayed in a movie starring Robin Williams. Patch believes in the healing power of happiness. Health care should emphasize caring.

I was inspired by Patch's talk. It was all about love and connection: How we can heal each other simply by opening our hearts and showing compassion. Medical training is just a bonus. His model of health care is based in clowning: Laughter and love can break down many barriers. I was so enchanted with these seemingly revolutionary ideas, I drove 60 miles to see him speak again the very next day.

That happened about the same time as I ended a tumultuous two-year relationship. I felt so liberated that I decided to join Patch Adams and a team of volunteers in Peru for two weeks after graduation. We visited nursing homes, shelters, orphanages, prisons, schools, and hospitals. We painted houses, and taught classes in dance, art, music, and health education. Afterward, I backpacked around Peru solo for two months.

The trip reinstated my faith in humans and provided hope for a system of genuine healing. I was amazed how helping others, even when I thought I had nothing to give, actually healed me.

The experience of releasing my fears to go into an impoverished village—where armed theft is a daily occurrence and children with dirty little bodies wear tattered clothes—and simply love every person I saw was empowering. Germ-theory be damned. The long hugs, laughter shared with strangers, and giving myself completely to a project beyond myself, healed wounds I didn't realize I had from living in a fiercely competitive and individualistic society.

Rachel Olsson is currently pursuing her passion of facilitating peaceful and empowering birth experiences by becoming a midwife.

chapter 5

craving comfort

There's nothing wrong
with crawling into bed with
Ben & Jerry, a spoon, and your remote
control, but here are some better ideas.

mushroom-smothered chicken with pasta

Makes 4 servings.

¼ cup all-purpose flour

½ teaspoon salt

¼ teaspoon ground black pepper

1½ pounds skinless, boneless chicken thighs
   and/or breasts

2 tablespoons olive oil

1 large onion, chopped

4 cups mushrooms *(shiitake, baby bellas,
   and/or morel if you are lucky enough to find
   them)*, halved

3 cloves garlic, minced

¾ cup dry white wine *(or chicken broth)*

¾ cup chicken broth

¼ cup snipped fresh herbs, such as oregano,
   basil, thyme, and/or parsley *(if you use only
   parsley, it will be a little bland)*

¼ cup cream or half-and-half

8 ounces linguine

¼ cup shredded provolone

1. In a plastic bag combine flour, salt, and black pepper. Add chicken pieces, a few at a time, shaking to coat. In a large skillet brown chicken in hot oil over medium-high heat for 3 to 4 minutes on each side. Remove chicken from skillet; set aside.

2. Add onions, mushrooms, and garlic. Cook for 5 minutes, stirring occasionally and scraping up any browned bits. Return chicken to pan. Add white wine, broth, and herbs. Bring to boiling; reduce heat. Cover and simmer for 20 minutes. Meanwhile, cook linguine according to package directions; drain.

3. Remove chicken from skillet; cover and keep warm. Add cream and gently simmer sauce, uncovered, for 5 minutes. Serve chicken and sauce over linguine. Sprinkle with provolone.

more-loose-than-sloppy joes

Makes 4 to 6 sandwiches, depending on how sloppy you make 'em.

1 pound lean ground beef *(85% to 90% lean)*

½ cup chopped onion

2 to 3 tablespoons ketchup

1 tablespoon yellow mustard

1-2 tablespoons pickle juice *(don't be scared, it's delicious!)*

1 teaspoon Worcestershire sauce

½ teaspoon pepper

2 tablespoons finely chopped sweet onion

Dill pickle slices

American cheese slices

1. In a skillet cook the ground beef and onion in hot oil over medium heat for 4 to 5 minutes or until beef is brown. Drain grease. Add the ketchup, mustard, pickle juice, Worcestershire sauce, pepper, salt, and garlic powder. Cook and stir about 5 minutes or until combined and saucy. Serve on hamburger buns with finely chopped sweet onions, pickle slices, and cheese, if desired.

LOOSELY SPEAKING
These loose meat burgers are based loosely (hehe) on Maid-Rite sandwiches created in Muscatine, Iowa. They're pretty low-key on the flavor scale but are regional happiness inducers.

beef barley stew

Makes 8 servings.

1 pound beef stew meat

1 tablespoon olive oil

3 cups beef broth

2 cups water

1 cup chopped onion

1 cup sliced carrots

½ cup chopped celery

2 cloves garlic, minced

1 tablespoon Worcestershire sauce

1 teaspoon ground thyme

1 bay leaf

1 teaspoon salt

½ teaspoon pepper

2 cups fresh mushrooms, sliced

¾ cup quick-cooking barley

¼ cup Burgundy or red wine

1. In a large soup pot brown meat in hot oil. Drain fat. Add broth, water, onion, carrots, celery, garlic, Worcestershire, thyme, bay leaf, salt, and pepper. Bring to boiling. Reduce heat and simmer, covered, for 1 to 1¼ hours or until meat is tender.

2. Stir in mushrooms and barley. Cover and simmer for 10 minutes more or until barley is tender. Stir in Burgundy just before serving.

fresh chunky tomato soup with pesto

Makes 4 servings.

1 large sweet onion, chopped

2 tablespoons butter

2 cloves garlic, minced

2 cups low-sodium chicken broth

6 large heirloom tomatoes, cored and chopped

¼ cup fresh basil leaves

Sea salt and freshly ground black pepper

4 teaspoons pesto

1. Cook onion in hot butter over medium heat for 4 to 5 minutes, stirring occasionally, until onion begins to soften. Add garlic. Cook and stir for 1 minute. Stir in broth, tomatoes, basil, salt, and pepper. Simmer, covered, for 25 minutes.

2. Cool slightly. Put half the soup in blender. Cover and blend until smooth. Stir blended soup into chunky soup in pot. Top each serving with a bit of pesto.

obnoxiously cheesy (and easy) mac 'n' cheese

Makes 2 servings.

½ cup elbow macaroni

1 tablespoon butter

¼ cup milk

½ cup shredded extra sharp cheddar cheese
   (or ¼ cup extra sharp cheddar plus ¼ cup
   smoked Gouda or your favorite cheese)

2 to 3 slices individually wrapped
   American cheese

1. Cook macaroni in a small saucepan according to package directions. Drain. Put drained macaroni back into saucepan.

2. Add butter, milk, and cheeses to pan. Stir over medium-low heat until the cheese is melted and the sauce is creamy and thick.

American cheese is a processed cheese that melts easily and makes this dish especially creamy. Think Velveeta or Kraft Singles.

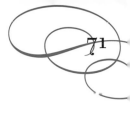

ooey-gooey grilled cheese sandwich

Makes 1 sandwich.

2 slices 7-grain bread *(about ½ inch thick)*

2 to 3 ounces sharp cheddar cheese, sliced

3 slices bacon, crisp-cooked

1. Put the cheese and bacon between bread slices. Heat 1 tablespoon butter in a skillet over medium heat and add sandwich. Cook about 2 to 3 minutes on each side, or until golden brown.

We know. Who needs a recipe for grilled cheese? No one. But it's one of our favorite comfort foods. Make it your own by playing with different cheeses. Slather pesto sauce on the bread before topping with cheese. Add a couple of thin slices of apple, pear, or tomato.

seriously easy roast chicken

Makes 8 servings.

1 4- to 5-pound whole chicken
¼ cup unsalted butter, softened
2 cloves garlic, minced
2 tablespoons snipped fresh rosemary or
   2 teaspoons crushed dried rosemary
1 teaspoon ground thyme
½ of a lemon, cut in wedges
½ of a small onion, cut in wedges
Salt and freshly ground black pepper

1. Preheat oven to 375°F. Stir together butter, garlic, rosemary, and thyme. Slather butter mixture on chicken, inside and out *(but mostly out)*. Squirt lemon juice from wedges over chicken. Tuck squeezed wedges into cavity along with onion wedges. Sprinkle with salt and pepper.

2. Place chicken, breast side up, on a rack in a roasting pan. Roast for 1½ to 2 hours, or until chicken is no longer pink and temperature is 180°F in meaty part of thigh. Let chicken rest for 15 minutes before slicing.

veggie-packed meat loaf

Makes 8 servings.

1 onion, chopped

1 carrot, chopped

½ of a red bell pepper, chopped

1 tablespoon cooking oil

2 cloves garlic, minced

2 cups (handfuls) fresh baby spinach

¼ teaspoon salt

¼ teaspoon ground black pepper

1 pound ground turkey

1 pound ground pork

½ cup Italian seasoned bread crumbs

2 eggs, room temperature

4 tablespoons ketchup, divided

1 teaspoon spicy brown mustard

1. Preheat oven to 350°F. In a skillet cook onion, carrot, and bell pepper in hot oil over medium heat for 5 minutes. Remove from heat. Stir in garlic, spinach, salt, and pepper.

2. In a large bowl mix together turkey, pork, bread crumbs, eggs, and 2 tablespoons of the ketchup. Add the cooked vegetables and mix until combined. Put mixture into an 8x4x2-inch loaf pan.

3. Bake for 1 to 1¼ hours or until meat loaf reaches 160°F. Carefully pour off fat. Meanwhile, stir together remaining 2 tablespoons ketchup and mustard; spread over meat loaf during last 10 minutes of baking. Remove from oven and let stand for 10 minutes before cutting.

Because we're feta cheese freaks, we usually toss ½ cup of feta cheese crumbles in with the meat loaf mixture before patting in the pan.

shepherd's porky pie

Makes 6 to 8 servings.

1 pound ground pork

1 medium onion, chopped

2 large carrots, chopped

1 green bell pepper, chopped

1 stalk celery, chopped

2 cloves garlic, minced

2 tablespoons ketchup

2 teaspoons soy sauce

1 teaspoon *(several good hearty dashes)* **Worcestershire sauce**

1 teaspoon Sriracha *(can you tell Lindsey loves this spicy Asian chili sauce? Use hot sauce or sprinkle in a few crushed red pepper flakes if you'd rather)*

½ teaspoon dried thyme

2 to 3 cups warm Garlic Mashed Potatoes *(see recipe, next page)*

1. Preheat oven to 350°F. In a large skillet, cook the pork and vegetables over medium heat, breaking apart the pork as it cooks with a wooden spoon. Keep going until the pork is browned and the vegetables are tender. Drain excess fat.

2. Now toss in your seasonings: a squirt of ketchup, soy sauce, Worcestershire, Sriracha, and thyme.

3. Pile the pork and vegetable mixture into a 2-quart casserole dish. Spread Garlic Mashed Potatoes on top like frosting. Bake for about 30 minutes, or until heated through and bubbly.

garlic mashed potatoes

Makes 4 to 6 servings.

2 to 2½ pounds baking potatoes, quartered

2 cloves garlic, squished through a garlic press

¼ cup butter

½ cup heavy cream (*half-and-half or milk works, too*)

1 teaspoon kosher salt

¼ teaspoon ground black pepper

Freshly grated Parmesan cheese (*optional*)

1. Put potatoes in a large saucepan (*toss a couple of extra peeled garlic cloves into the water if you want to keep the vampires at bay*). Cover with water and sprinkle generously with salt. Bring to boiling. Reduce heat and simmer, covered, about 20 minutes or until tender; drain.

2. Meanwhile, in a small skillet, cook garlic in hot butter over low heat about 3 minutes or until garlic is tender. Gently mash potatoes. Add butter mixture, cream, salt, and pepper; mash until soft and fluffy. Sprinkle with cheese, if you like.

THE CARB CURE
Yup. Carbohydrates are powerful stress busters. The tension-taming impact is due to serotonin—the feel-good chemical—which is triggered by carb-rich foods. We know from personal experience that mashed potatoes induce a relaxation response. Be sure to add complex carbs—such as whole grain breads, pastas, and cereals—to your diet. A piece of whole grain toast at bedtime may help you doze off quickly.

kick-ass guajillo-sauced enchiladas

Guajillo Chile Sauce *(next page)*

⅓ cup half-and-half or coconut milk

2 medium shallots or 1 small onion, chopped

2 tablespoons butter

1 package baby bella mushrooms, sliced

3 tablespoons of tomato puree

2 tablespoons red wine *(optional but tasty)*

2 to 3 cloves garlic, minced

3 cups fresh spinach

8 corn tortillas

½ cup cotija, goat cheese, or
   Monterey Jack *(or even no cheese at all)*

1. In a small saucepan heat Guajillo Chile Sauce over medium heat just until it begins to bubble. Remove from heat and stir in half-and-half; set aside.

2. In a wok or large skillet cook shallots in hot butter over medium heat until onions soften. Add mushrooms; cook and stir for 4 minutes or until they soften. Add tomato puree, wine *(if desired)*, and garlic. Cook and stir for 3 minutes. Add 2 tablespoons of the guajillo mixture and finally, the spinach. Cook and stir until wilted and heated through.

3. Put remaining guajillo mixture in a shallow pan. Dip tortillas in mixture, then sear in hot oil in a cast-iron skillet on medium-high heat for about 30 seconds *(just one side)*. Top tortilla with tasty mushroom-spinach filling; roll tortillas around filling. Drizzle with sauce and sprinkle with cheese. Serve immediately, one by one. Better yet, create an assembly line and hand your guests a sizzling tortilla *(on a plate, of course)*, point them to the mushroom-spinach mixture, guajillo mixture, and cheese, and let them roll their own.

4. Or preheat oven to 400°F. Place rolled tortillas in a 13x9-inch baking pan *(skip the oil searing if you're feeling lazy; we often do)*. Drizzle with guajillo mixture and sprinkle with cheese. Bake for 10 minutes or until heated through.

guajillo chile sauce

4 to 5 dried guajillo chile peppers or any
    dried chiles
½ cup liquid from peppers
2 to 4 tablespoons tomato puree
1-2 cloves garlic, smashed with knife
    and peeled
1 tablespoon canola or olive oil

1. Snap off and discard stems of chiles. Tear them open and shake out and discard seeds (*keep the seeds for a spicy sauce*). Cover chiles with boiling hot water; soak for 10 to 20 minutes or until they soften.

2. In a blender combine soaked guajillo peppers, water, tomato puree, garlic, and oil. (*Add more tomato puree to taste. We like ours heavy on the chiles.*) It should be the consistency of thick tomato juice. Pour sauce in a saucepan and simmer for 5 minutes.

This is a kicky all-purpose sauce, great to mix into salsas, pep up scrambled eggs or fried rice, or as a marinade for pork or chicken.

over the moon chocolate chip cookies

Makes 2 to 3 dozen.

1 cup flour

½ teaspoon baking soda

½ teaspoon salt

¼ teaspoon baking powder

½ cup unsalted butter, softened

½ cup brown sugar

½ cup granulated sugar

1 teaspoon vanilla extract

1 egg

1 cup chocolate chips

1 cup coarsely chopped high-quality dark bittersweet chocolate

¾ cup coarsely chopped walnuts

Sea salt

1. Preheat oven to 350°F. Combine flour, baking soda, salt, and baking powder. *(Be sure baking powder and soda are mixed well with the flour, otherwise you'll get funky white spots in your final cookie.)*

2. With a mixer, cream butter, sugars, and vanilla until light and fluffy. *(Don't rush. It may take up to 5 minutes.)* Add egg, and mix well. Gradually beat in flour mixture until just combined. *(You may have to turn your mixer to low. And don't overbeat.)* Use a spoon to stir in chocolate and walnuts. Press a sheet of plastic wrap over dough and stash it in the fridge overnight. *(If you're impatient go ahead to the next step, but bake for only 10 to 12 minutes.)*

3. When ready to bake, scoop heaping—really heaping—tablespoons of chilled dough onto ungreased baking sheets. Sprinkle with sea salt. Bake for 12 to 15 minutes or until golden brown. Cool for 5 minutes before moving cookies to a wire rack to cool a little longer, but be sure to eat one or two while warm.

chunks o' chocolate and strawberry frozen yogurt

Makes about 1 quart

3 cups Greek-style yogurt
½ cup sugar
2 cups fresh strawberries or raspberries
⅓ cup coarsely chopped dark chocolate

1. Combine yogurt, sugar and 1 cup of the strawberries. Blend until almost smooth. Pour mixture into ice cream freezer container.

2. Freeze according to manufacturer's directions. Take out dasher. Slice remaining strawberries. Stir slice berries and chocolate into the frozen yogurt. Texture is best when eaten immediately. Or store, covered in the freezer. Before serving, let stand at room temperature for 10 minutes to soften.

chapter 6

garden therapy

Hanging out with plants takes away
so many woes. The aromatherapy is divine.
And sometimes you've just got to stop
and eat the roses.

it's-greek-to-me salad

Makes 4 servings.

6 cups torn romaine lettuce leaves or
    mixed greens

3 medium tomatoes, cut into wedges

2 medium cucumbers, peeled and
    coarsely chopped

1 small red onion, cut into thin wedges

1 6-ounce jar marinated artichoke hearts,
    drained and coarsely chopped

Herb Vinaigrette *(right)*

½ cup pitted kalamata olives

½ cup shredded mizithra cheese or crumbled
    feta cheese

1. In a salad bowl combine lettuce, tomatoes, cucumbers, onion, and artichoke hearts. Add Herb Vinaigrette; toss to coat. Sprinkle with olives and cheese.

Herb Vinaigrette: In a screw-top jar combine ¼ cup olive oil; 3 tablespoons lemon juice; 1 clove garlic, minced; 1 teaspoon fresh oregano, chopped; 1 teaspoon fresh basil or thyme, chopped; and a dash of salt and freshly ground black pepper. Shake it, baby.

green goddess jealous aphrodite dip

Makes about 1 cup of dressing/dip.

½ cup light mayonnaise

¼ cup light sour cream

2 tablespoons chopped green onions or chives

2 tablespoons parsley, chopped

1 tablespoon lime juice *(or try tarragon vinegar)*

1 tablespoon watercress, chopped

1 teaspoon fresh tarragon, snipped

1 fillet white anchovy, minced

1 clove garlic, minced

Dippers such as chunks of sourdough bread;
   pita wedges, snow peas, cucumber slices,
   and/or red and orange sweet pepper chunks

1. Whisk all of the ingredients, except dippers, together. Then dip in. *(Or thin it out with a bit of milk and you've got a dressing for salads.)*

Tarragon is traditional in green goddess dressing, but you can use it or lose it. Lindsey's not a fan.

over-the-rainbow chard pasta

Makes 4 servings.

8 ounces fusilli or linguine, broken in half

2 medium tomatoes, chopped

2 medium summer squash or zucchini, halved
   and cut in ½-inch slices

3 cloves garlic, minced

3 tablespoons butter

2 tablespoons olive oil

¼ teaspoon red pepper flakes

4 to 5 cups roughly chopped rainbow chard

2 teaspoons fresh chopped rosemary

1 tablespoon fresh chopped basil

½ cup grated Asiago or Parmesan cheese

1. Cook pasta according to package directions. Meanwhile, in a Dutch oven cook tomatoes, squash, garlic, and chile pepper flakes in hot butter and olive oil over medium heat for 3 to 4 minutes, or until crisp-tender. Add rainbow chard and rosemary, tossing, stirring, and cooking for 5 to 10 minutes, or until chard wilts. (The bigger the pot, the quicker the chard will wilt. Pile veggie mixture all over pasta. Shower it with cheese.

poblano pepper slaw with citrus dressing

Makes 4 servings.

3 tablespoons mayonnaise

3 tablespoons fresh squeezed orange juice

1 tablespoon lime juice

1 tablespoon minced green onion

1 to 2 teaspoons sugar *(taste the dressing to see if it's sweet-tart enough for you)*

¼ teaspoon salt

¼ teaspoon freshly ground black pepper

4 cups thinly sliced cabbage

1 avocado, peeled, seeded, and coarsely chopped

½ of a fresh poblano pepper, seeded and minced *(or sweet banana pepper for a mellow kick)*

1 tablespoon cilantro, chopped

1. In a small bowl, make citrus dressing by whisking together mayonnaise, orange juice, lime juice, green onion, salt, and pepper.

2. In a large bowl, gently toss cabbage, avocado, poblano pepper, cilantro, and citrus dressing.

FLOWER POWER
Look at flowers first thing in the morning to feel more cheery and energetic throughout the day. The power of scent and color can both relax and brighten mood, according to a Harvard Medical School and Massachusetts General Hospital study.

super-fast shrimp, spinach, and bow-ties

Serves 4.

8 ounces dried farfalle (bow-tie pasta)

½ cup pesto

12 ounces cooked shrimp

3 cups fresh baby spinach, thinly sliced

2 tablespoons pitted oil-cured black olives

2 tablespoons chopped fresh basil

2 tablespoons freshly grated Parmesan cheese

1. Cook farfalle according to package directions. Meanwhile, in a small saucepan, heat pesto just until warm, stirring frequently.

2. Put shrimp in colander. Drain pasta over shrimp *(just to warm up the cooked shrimp)*. In a large bowl, combine pasta, shrimp, pesto, olives, and basil. Toss to combine. Shower with cheese.

total satisfaction salad

Makes 4 main-dish servings.

Easy Vinaigrette (*below right*)

1 to 2 tablespoons Cajun seasoning

½ cup fine dry bread crumbs

4 catfish (or tilapia) fillets

2 tablespoons olive oil

8 cups mixed spring greens (bagged salad works well)

2 ounces crumbled blue cheese or coarsely shredded white cheddar cheese

¼ cup pecans, toasted

4 slices Candied Bacon *(recipe, page 15)*, cut into large pieces or crumbled

1. Make Easy Vinaigrette. Set aside.

2. Mix Cajun seasoning with bread crumbs. Press crumb mixture onto catfish fillets. Heat olive oil in a very large skillet. Add catfish and cook for 4 to 6 minutes per ½-inch thickness of fish or until it flakes when you poke it with a fork, turning once.

3. Put 2 cups of greens on each of four plates. Top with a catfish fillet, blue cheese, pecans, and Candied Bacon. Drizzle with Easy Vinaigrette.

Easy Vinaigrette: In a screw-top jar combine 2 tablespoons olive oil, 2 tablespoons vinegar, 1 teaspoon brown sugar or honey, ½ teaspoon Dijon mustard, and a sprinkling of salt and pepper. Shake, shake, shake. (Remember to screw the lid on first.)

mexican street corn

Makes 4 servings.

2 tablespoons butter

1 tablespoon minced sweet banana pepper
   (or skip the pepper)

1 clove garlic, minced

¼ cup mayonnaise

4 ears fresh sweet corn, husked

4 lime wedges

½ cup crumbled cotija or queso fresco cheese
   *(feta works too, but then you'll have to call
   this Greek corn)*

Chipotle chile powder

1. In a small skillet combine butter, banana pepper, and garlic. Cook over low heat until butter is melted and garlic begins to soften. Cool slightly. Stir in mayonnaise.

2. Grill corn on a charcoal grill for 10 to 12 minutes or until corn begins to turn golden brown, turning frequently.

3. Rub each ear of corn with a lime wedge, then slather with mayonnaise mixture, and sprinkle generously with cheese and subtly with chipotle powder. *(Or hand over the grilled naked ears and have everyone fancy up their own.)*

caprese-stye bacon, lettuce, and tomato sandwich

Makes 6 servings.

1 10-inch round focaccia bread, split in half horizontally so you have a top half and a bottom half (*a serrated knife works best for this*)

2 to 4 tablespoons butter, softened

¾ cup mayonnaise

Juice of ½ a lemon

12 slices thick-cut pepper bacon, cooked until crispy

2 ripe avocados, peeled, pitted, and sliced

2 to 3 large heirloom tomatoes, thickly sliced

Sea salt and freshly ground black pepper

10 to 12 fresh basil leaves

1 to 2 cups spring greens

6 mini balls oil-packed herb bocconcini, drained and sliced (*or sliced fresh mozzarella works too*)

1. Preheat oven to 400°F. Place both halves of focaccia bread on a large baking sheet with cut side up. Brush cut sides of bread with butter. Bake for 5 minutes or until focaccia is crispy on edges and hot.

2. Meanwhile stir together mayonnaise and lemon juice. When focaccia is toasted, spread mayonnaise mixture on cut sides of bread. Top one side with bacon, avocados, and tomato slices; sprinkle tomato with sea salt and pepper. Add basil, greens, and herb bocconcini. Top with remaining focaccia half. Cut into 6 wedges.

Renee Schettler Rossi, New York City

the secret ingredient

My Grandma Huegerich was a recipe clipper. I remember being not yet five years old, standing on a chair in front of her kitchen counter, a flour sack towel tied around my tummy. She would stand beside me in her flowered cotton housedress, straps sliding off her shoulder, the most recent newspaper clipping before us.

She was a calming presence in the kitchen, her motions as slow and certain and mesmerizing as the drone of the cicadas outside the screen door. Her deeply tanned, gently wrinkled, knowing hands moved expertly above the glitter laminate counter, always at the same unhurried pace. She tried to act as though baking was just another chore, but each time we tried something new, her anticipation was tangible. And then: the tasting. The pause. And her sing-songy exclamation that I can hear in my head to this day: "Ohhhh, that's so gooood!" The look in her eyes and the lilt in her voice said it all.

She and I shared a wanderlust that wasn't confined to the kitchen. While I sent her postcards from Europe, she captured recipes for me in a simple spiralbound notebook. By the time I was a writer and editor on the East Coast, she was ill. Yet she continued writing in that lovely, shaky penmanship. At times there were no instructions, only lists of ingredients, it was all so intuitive. "For my granddaughter, the food writer," she'd tell everyone who would listen.

My notebook, which she handed to me from her hospice bed, comprised 30 recipes. They were mostly baked goods, with names like "Delicious Cookies" and "Two Hour Buns," and endearing insights such as "My Favorite" that still make me sigh. As usual, she was spare with her words. There was no sentimental inscription, not even a signature. The recipes simply started on page three with her pie crust. The full expression of her love, however, could be found a few pages later with her legendary recipe for peach pie, which many had coveted but no one had glimpsed. This is my legacy, I thought, imagining my children one day knowing their great grandmother through her impossibly flaky pastry, her peaches sliced just so, the runny yet clingy filling unfettered with spice yet rich with just the right amount of ... well, I'm not supposed to tell.

When she passed, everyone extolled her even temperament, her capacity to see the best in others as well as in life, despite inevitable disappointment. That was her way. I, unlike her, started to see the worst, not in people but in the recipes I tested and tweaked and rejected with a vengeance each day. Nothing measured up.

This sentiment seemed to be shared by my 94-year-old grandfather. On more than one occasion he was caught sneaking out to the store to fetch the makings for a simple ham sandwich. After 64 years of Grandma's cooking, he'd gruffly made known that the inept kitchen skills of an unfamiliar caretaker simply weren't tolerable.

It took time for me to understand that it wasn't peach pie that he and I needed. Or any of those other carefully inscribed recipes. It was her day-to-day cooking, practical and perfect. Mornings were henhouse eggs over easy, bacon crisped at the edges, and her strawberry jam on homemade bread. Midday meant pot roast, potatoes dug from the garden, then boiled, and more jelly bread. Supper was, in a savvy manner of speaking, leftovers. Beef warmed in its juices took its place alongside boiled potatoes sliced and sizzled in bacon drippings from the tin coffee can alongside the stove. It was simple, familiar food, done thriftily and perfectly. That, I know now, is my legacy.

Renee Schettler Rossi, who has written and edited at Real Simple, Martha Stewart Living, *and* The Washington Post, *has danced around heartbreak of all sorts.*

chapter 7

life ain't no picnic

unless you make it one

Have a pouting picnic anywhere.
Any time. Solo or with friends.
It'll take your mind off
any life-altering pratfall.

watermelon salad with cotija cheese

Makes about 3 servings *(although Jeanne downed the whole bowl as her lunch one day).*

2 cups watermelon chunks

2 tablespoons snipped fresh herbs *(we used parsley and chocolate mint because that's what was abundant in our garden; cilantro and basil are good options, too)*

1 teaspoon key lime juice or lime or lemon juice

1 teaspoon olive oil

Sea salt

Freshly ground black pepper

2 tablespoons crumbled cotija or feta cheese *(any salty, crumbly cheese will do)*

2 tablespoons roasted pepitas* or sunflower seeds *(or any coarsely chopped toasted nut)*

1. Toss everything except pepitas and cheese in a bowl. Sprinkle with nuts and cheese just before serving.

2. If you're toting this to a picnic, carry the nuts and cheese in separate containers or plastic bags until ready to use.

*Pepitas are the kernels of pumpkin seeds. So delish.

crunchy apple salad

Makes 4 servings.

2 tart green apples, cored and chopped

16 grapes, halved

2 tablespoons sliced almonds or coarsely chopped pecans

1 tablespoon dried cranberries or dried blueberries

Balsamic vinaigrette or raspberry vinaigrette

Salt and pepper

1. In a small bowl, combine fruit and nuts. Drizzle with vinaigrette. Sprinkle with salt and pepper. Toss to combine.

CHEESY DOES IT
Happiness experts insist that just simulating a smile triggers your brain to lift your mood. So when nobody's looking, try:
- Saying cheese over and over, or just the "eeee"
- Keeping a pencil lengthwise between your upper and lower teeth
- Catching yourself in the mirror as you perform the above (you just might smile for real)

feta potato salad

Makes 4 to 6 servings.

1½ pounds small red new potatoes or Yukon gold potatoes *(cut large potatoes in quarters)*

3 eggs

¾ cup mayonnaise

½ cup sour cream

1 tablespoon Dijon mustard *(or whatever's in the fridge)*

Salt and freshly ground black pepper

1 cup crumbled feta cheese *(more if you're lovin' it)*

⅓ cup coarsely chopped, pitted kalamata olives *(optional)*

1. Cook potatoes. You know how to do that right? Put 'em in a pan; cover with water. Crank up the heat until water boils. Reduce heat and simmer, covered, for 20 minutes or until tender *(just poke one with a fork to test)*. Drain. Cool.

2. Meanwhile, get the eggs going. Put eggs in a small saucepan, and cover with water. Bring to boiling. Remove pan from heat and cover. Let eggs stand for 15 minutes. Drain and cool in cold water. Cut potatoes and eggs into bite-size chunks.

3. Stir together the mayo, sour cream, and Dijon.

4. In a big bowl combine potatoes, eggs, mayo mixture, salt, and pepper. Toss gently to coat. Cover and place in refrigerator for 1 to 24 hours *(or proceed directly to step 5)*.

5. Just before serving, stir in feta cheese and olives, if you wish.

Potato salad is pretty versatile. Toss in whatever sounds good. Jeanne adds half a small sweet onion, chopped. Lindsey likes chopped garlic scapes or minced garlic and chopped red sweet pepper. Throw in some capers, parsley, or basil.

deli chicken with blue cheese dunking sauce

Makes 4 servings.

4 ounces cream cheese, softened

4 ounces crumbled Cambozola* or other
blue cheese

1 to 3 teaspoons white wine, cream, or milk

1 tablespoon chopped pecans or
walnuts, toasted

1 3-pound deli-roasted chicken *(or a bucket of*
grilled chicken from you know where)

Crunchy vegetables, such as celery,
cucumbers, and/or carrots *(so you'll feel*
somewhat healthful)

1. Make a dipping sauce by combining cream cheese, Cambozola, and wine. Use a fork to stir it together until it's creamy but still slightly thick. Add more wine, if needed, to thin out the sauce. Stir in pecans. Cover and chill.

2. Load up your picnic basket. Don't forget the Cambozola cheese mixture. Get in your car. Stop at the grocery store, or drive-through your favorite fried/grilled chicken joint. Grab chicken. Cut it up when you get to your picnic spot. *(Or use your clean fingers to tear into it.)* Pass the Cambozola sauce or slather it on top of each piece.

3. The dunking sauce goes well with crunchy veggies too.

*Cambozola is a mild, creamy blue cheese that is sometimes called blue brie.

white bean tuna salad

Makes 4 to 6 servings.

1 15-ounce can cannellini beans, rinsed and drained
1 6-ounce can solid white tuna in water, drained
1 stalk celery, finely chopped
1 shallot, finely chopped
1 clove garlic, minced
½ of a lemon
2 tablespoons olive oil
2 tablespoons mayonnaise
Salt and pepper

1. In a medium bowl combine beans, tuna, celery, shallot, and garlic. Squeeze the lemon half over the mixture. Drizzle with the olive oil, then add mayo, salt, and pepper. Mix it all up.

2. Use the mixture to make sandwiches *(focaccia bread or ciabatta rolls would be great),* or pile salad greens on individual plates and top each plate o' greens with a scoop of the tuna mixture.

THE TUNA TUNE
For kicks, do a Google search for the "Slap Chop Rap," and listen to it while you whip up this picnic spread. As the infamous Vince Offer sings/slaps/raps: "Stop having a boring tuna. Stop having a boring life!"

lazy-day mudslide brownies

Makes about 20 brownies.

1 package family-style fudge brownie mix
   (we like Duncan Hines)
2 eggs
½ cup butter, melted
¼ mudslide mix
¼ cup bittersweet chocolate chips

1. Preheat oven to 350°F. Line a 13x9x2 pan with foil *(or for thicker brownies, use a 9x9x2-inch pan)*, leaving an overhang on opposite sides. Grease foil with butter.

2. Combine brownie mix, eggs, melted butter, and mudslide mix in a large bowl. Stir with a spoon until well mixed. Stir in chocolate chips. Spoon into pan and spread evenly.

3. Bake about 30 minutes *(or if using 9x9x2-inch pan, bake about 35 minutes)* or until toothpick inserted in center comes out clean. Cool on a wire rack. Carefully lift out the foil along with the slab of brownies. Remove foil and cut brownies into bars.

jasmine mint tea

Makes about ½ gallon.

6 cups water, brought just to boiling

4 jasmine tea bags

2 peppermint tea bags

**1 tablespoon honey (*Jeanne skips the honey,*
    —she's not a sweet person)**

4 cups ice

Lemon slices

Fresh mint sprigs

1. Steep tea and honey in hot water for 5 to 6 minutes *(longer if you want a stronger flavor)*. Remove tea bags. Cool. Pour into a pitcher over ice. Serve in ice-filled glasses with lemon slices and mint sprigs. Keeps up to 3 days in the refrigerator.

Sheena Chihak, Des Moines, Iowa

soothed by spontaneity

The heartbreak of losing a parent became a reality for me at age 20 when my father died. My younger siblings were just 18, 17, and 12 and suddenly Dad was gone. The loss was gut-wrenching.

On the drive home from my dad's visitation, my mom veered into the parking lot of a somewhat seedy grocery store. She hustled us inside, telling us we were on a junk food spree. Like kids in a candy store, we all went crazy and walked out with armloads of chips, chocolate, and sweets galore.

For my health-conscious mother, this binge was truly surprising. Just for a moment we were throwing everything we knew about junk food and its unhealthiness out the window.

And it wasn't so much the eating of the food that cheered us, but the process. We all giggled ourselves to tears, especially after we realized how we must've looked to the regular customers—an entire dressed-up family with a major case of the munchies.

It was this simple, spur-of-the-moment idea that started our anguished family on the path to healing. The experience made us laugh, something our family hadn't done since Dad died. It was the best release possible. I knew life would never be the same, but to this day that silly shopping spree reminds me to live, live, live in the moment.

Sheena Chihak is a registered dietitian and food editor/writer.

chapter 8

grills only

Who says slapping a steak
on the 'que is a guy thing?
Whip out your Weber (or whatever)
and watch your woes
sizzle into oblivion.

coffee buzzed sliders

Makes 8 mini burgers (4 servings).

2 tablespoons freshly ground coffee *(not pre-ground or instant)*

2 teaspoons packed brown sugar

1 teaspoon ground coriander

½ teaspoon kosher salt

½ teaspoon freshly ground black pepper

½ teaspoon dried oregano, crushed

⅛ teaspoon cayenne pepper

⅛ teaspoon ground cinnamon

2 cloves garlic, minced

1 pound ground chuck

Cheese *(for a super-caffeinated slider, add Barely Buzzed cheese; it's a sharp cheese with an espresso-rubbed rind. See* **beehivecheese.com***)*

8 dinner rolls or mini burger buns

Condiments of your choice

1. In a small bowl combine coffee, brown sugar, coriander, salt, pepper, oregano, cayenne pepper, and cinnamon.

2. Mix about half of the coffee rub and the garlic into the ground chuck. Form into eight 2-ounce patties. Coat each patty with a sprinkling of the coffee rub.

3. Heat a large skillet over medium-high heat. Add patties and cook about 8 to 9 minutes or until done *(about 160°F)*, turning once halfway through cooking. Or grill on a grill rack over medium coals for about 9 to 10 minutes, turning once. When sliders are almost done, top with cheese. Place sliders on buns and add condiments.

You can also use this rub on steaks. It rocks.

like-a-gyro turkey burger

Makes 4 servings.

¼ cup fine dry bread crumbs

½ teaspoon dried oregano or marjoram

½ teaspoon ground cumin

2 cloves garlic, minced

¼ teaspoon salt

¼ teaspoon cayenne pepper

1 pound uncooked ground turkey

2 tablespoons plain yogurt

4 hamburger buns, split and toasted

Tzatziki (see below right)

½ cup fresh spinach

1. In a bowl stir up the bread crumbs, marjoram, garlic, salt, and cayenne pepper. Add the turkey and yogurt and mash it together with your hands. Pat into four ¾-inch-thick patties.

2. Grill on a grill rack directly over medium heat for 14 to 18 minutes or until no longer pink (165°F), turning once halfway through grilling. Or heat 1 tablespoon cooking oil and 1 tablespoon butter in a large skillet over medium-high heat. Add burgers and cook for 14 to 18 minutes, turning once.

3. Serve burgers on toasted buns with Tzatziki and spinach.

Tzatziki: In a small bowl combine ½ cup shredded or finely chopped cucumber, ½ cup Greek yogurt, 1 to 2 tablespoons chopped chives or red onions, 1 teaspoon lemon juice, and ¼ teaspoon salt.

Greek yogurt will change your life. It's rich, creamy and dee-licious. Take it to breakfastland or dessertville and drizzle it with honey, sprinkle with nuts and/or granola, and fresh berries.

ribeye steaks with horseradish chive butter

Makes 4 servings.

¼ cup butter, softened

1 tablespoon prepared horseradish *(add*
   1 extra teaspoon if you like it potent)

1 clove garlic, minced

2 teaspoons chopped chives or shallots

¼ teaspoon coarse sea salt

¼ teaspoon cracked black pepper

4 beef ribeye steaks, cut 1 inch thick

1. Combine butter, horseradish, garlic, and chives in a small bowl; mix well. Cover and refrigerate until serving time.

2. Sprinkle both sides of steaks with salt and pepper. Grill over medium coals until it's done to your liking *(we recommend medium rare: 8 to 12 minutes)*, turning about halfway through. Put a dollop of horseradish butter on each piece. Cover and refrigerate remaining horseradish butter for 3 to 4 days. *(It's good on grilled cheese sandwiches or panini.)*

korean barbecued beef

Makes 6 servings.

1½ pounds boneless beef sirloin steak

6 tablespoons light soy sauce

3 green onions, chopped

3 cloves garlic, minced (1 tablespoon)

2 tablespoons brown sugar

1 tablespoon toasted sesame seeds

1 tablespoon grated fresh ginger

1 tablespoon toasted sesame oil

1 teaspoon crushed red pepper

Boston or butterhead lettuce leaves

Hot cooked rice

1. Put sirloin in a plastic bag and set it in a dish. Add the soy sauce, green onions, garlic, brown sugar, sesame seeds, ginger, sesame oil, and crushed red pepper. Zip the bag closed and jostle it around until the meat is coated. Marinate in the refrigerator for 4 to 24 hours; overnight is about right.

2. Remove sirloin from marinade and place on a grill rack over medium heat. Grill for 14 to 18 minutes, flipping halfway through. *(Use an instant-read meat thermometer: medium rare is 145°F; medium is 160°F.)*

3. Thinly slice the sirloin. Top lettuce leaves with rice and sliced sirloin.

tropical salmon salad with mango and avocado

Makes 4 servings.

2 4-ounce skinless salmon fillets, about
   1 inch thick
1 tablespoon olive oil
1 tablespoon lime juice *(or lemon juice)*
Salt and pepper
6 cups torn mixed greens
1 medium avocado, halved, seeded, peeled,
   and sliced
1 medium mango, seeded, peeled, and sliced
Coconut Lime Dressing *(right)*
3 tablespoons chopped macadamia nuts
   (or peanuts)

1. Brush fish with oil and sprinkle with lime juice, salt, and pepper. Grill on a greased rack over medium coals 8 to 12 minutes or until fish flakes easily, turning halfway through. Cut fish into bite-size pieces.

2. In a large salad bowl, toss together greens, avocado, and mango; toss gently to mix. Drizzle with Coconut Lime Dressing; toss again. Divide salad among 4 plates. Top with grilled salmon and macadamia nuts.

Coconut Lime Dressing: Whisk together 2 tablespoons unsweetened coconut milk, 2 tablespoons lime juice, 1 tablespoon peanut butter, 1 teaspoon honey, 1 clove minced garlic, ½ teaspoon salt, and ¼ teaspoon Asian chile sauce. Add 1 to 3 teaspoons water, if needed, to make the dressing thin enough to drizzle over salad.

furikake-crusted tuna steaks

Makes 4 servings.

4 5- to 6-ounce tuna steaks, about
   1 inch thick

3 tablespoons low-sodium soy sauce

3 tablespoons sesame chili oil *(or*
   1½ tablespoons sesame oil and
   ½ tablespoon Sriracha or hot sauce)

1 tablespoon lemon juice

2 to 3 tablespoons furikake *(or sesame seeds)*

1. Put fish in a plastic bag set in a dish or pie plate. Add the soy sauce, sesame chili oil, and lemon juice. Zip the bag closed and jostle it around until the fish is coated. Marinate it in the fridge for 15 to 20 minutes.

2. Remove fish from bag. Sprinkle both sides of fish with furikake. Grill fish on greased rack over medium coals for 3 to 4 minutes on each side for seared rare deliciousness. If you're not into just-seared tuna, grill it for 4 to 6 minutes on each side or until it feels flaky when you poke around with a fork.

Furikake is a Japanese seasoning blend that often contains sesame seeds, chopped dried seaweed, bonito, powdered miso, and other goodies. Find it in Asian markets. Once you find it, you'll be sprinkling it on everything.

outrageous marinated veggie kabobs

Makes 4 servings.

7 to 8 ounces mini sweet peppers

16 grape or cherry tomatoes

1 cup zucchini chunks

6 green onions, cut in 2-inch pieces

¼ cup canola or olive oil

2 tablespoons low-sodium soy sauce

2 tablespoons lime juice

1 tablespoon fresh oregano, basil, or cilantro

2 cloves garlic, minced

1 teaspoon spicy brown mustard (or Dijon, if you prefer)

1. Put vegetables in a plastic bag. Add oil, soy sauce, lime juice, herb of choice, garlic, and mustard. Zip the bag closed and jostle it around until all the vegetables are coated. Marinate for at least 10 minutes and at most 45 minutes.

2. Remove veggies from marinade and thread onto skewers. If using wooden skewers, soak in water for a half hour prior to grilling. (*As you thrust the veggies onto the sticks, imagine all your woes being pierced, soon to be engulfed in flames, never to plague you again.*)

3. Place skewers on grill over medium high heat for 5 to 10 minutes or until crisp tender, turning every few minutes.

For a flavor explosion, thread chunks of banana pepper and pineapple onto the skewers with the veggies.

Paul G. Meesey, St. Louis, Missouri

heart to heart

Did you hear the one about the St. Louis man who settled into his seat at Powell Symphony Hall a month before his 52nd birthday when the unthinkable happened?

Aron Ralston, the speaker that evening, was about to share his story of perseverance and faith. Ralston was the climber who amputated his own arm after it was pinned by a boulder, trapping him in a Utah canyon for days. An accidental face to face with destiny. Walking one minute. Hopelessly trapped the next.

That night, 10 minutes before Ralston's introduction, I wipe my forehead with the pad of my hand, light-headed and uncomfortably warm from the hike to our mezzanine perch high above the red velvet sea of plush opera seats.

Waiting, panting, shifting in my seat, I slip out of my jacket and hope the lights would finally dim. Maybe the change in atmosphere, the introduction, the applause, might take my mind off the anxiety I was experiencing. Why had I guzzled that vodka and diet Sprite just before leaving the house? Why hadn't I eaten dinner?

And I'm sleepy, so sleepy. Suddenly, I snort, as if coming out of a nap. But instead of waking, I slump, leaning into my date who happens to be an ICU nurse at a small urban hospital.

Recognizing the "guppying" sound I was making—like a carp sucking in air while collecting food pellets on the water's surface—my date shoves me back. Nurses know that sound is made in the final moments of life.

My date helps me to the floor. I remember nothing. No jaw pain. No heavy weight in my chest. No searing ache in my arm. No panic. Just a familiar drifting off to sleep. I'd passed beyond consciousness and was not breathing, nor was my heart beating. I did not have an effective heartbeat for 13 minutes. Thirteen. The number 13 holds special meaning in my family. I am one of 13 siblings. My family can tell you countless reoccurrences of our "lucky" 13. Tonight it would be lucky again.

From several nearby seats, doctors appear. As one doctor begins rapid compressions on my barrel chest, my date tries to get some breaths into me. My head bucks and I bite her lip.

She calmly asks for oxygen, an AED *(automated external defibrillator)*, and a "cardiac ambulance." My shirt is opened and pads adhered to my chest and belly. One zap is delivered. Then another and another. The doc keeps pumping my ribs in between the paramedic's efforts to jump-start my heart with the AED.

By my side my date holds my hand and talks to me about my sons. She tells me I am not ready to leave them yet. And they are not ready to lose me.

The paramedic administers 10 shocks in all. Finally, 13 minutes after my heart stopped, my rhythm is restored. Although I felt as if I were engulfed in an impenetrable fog, I vaguely remember being embarrassed at the scene I was causing. And I wonder how the young firemen would cart me—and the guerney I was loaded on—down the seemingly endless flight of steps I'd climbed up less than half an hour earlier.

Thirteen minutes. I'd upstaged the guy who'd cut off his arm. The commotion I'd created delayed the show, if only for 13 minutes. I found out later that my anterior descending artery had been blocked. I died that night in November. And then I lived.

I'm thankful I returned to life with my mind and body relatively unscathed. I'm thankful for the three doctors who descended on me out of thin air, and for the AED that hung in a broom closet on MY side of the symphony hall. I'm thankful I had a date who knew me and who knew what to do. Most of all, I'm thankful that I have the rest of my life to appreciate my days, my nights, my sons, and my world so rich, so wonderful, so very special.

Paul G. Meesey is in Year Three of his comeback, enjoying the extra innings.

chapter 9

a bit boozy

Not that we're encouraging you to drink
yourself silly, but a splash of potent
potables adds a giddy sense of delight
to food and cocktails.

ale-cheddar soup with bacon croutons

Makes 6 cheesy servings.

1 cup chopped onion

½ cup chopped carrots *(about 2 carrots)*

½ cup chopped celery

1 jalapeño pepper, seeded and finely chopped

3 tablespoons butter

3 cloves garlic, minced

3 tablespoons flour

½ teaspoon dry mustard *(optional)*

1 14-ounce can low-sodium chicken broth

1 12-ounce bottle of ale *(Bud Light works, but then we'd have to change the name of the recipe)*

1 pint half-and-half or 2 cups milk

1 teaspoon Worcestershire sauce

3 to 4 cups shredded cheddar cheese *(we like to use smoked Gouda for half of the cheese)*

Bacon Croutons *(see right)*

1. Cook onion, carrots, celery, and jalapeño in hot butter over medium heat for about 10 minutes or until onions soften, stirring now and then. Add garlic and stir for 1 minute. Stir in flour and, if you like, dry mustard; cook and stir for 1 to 2 minutes until flour is all mixed in and thickens.

2. Slowly add half-and-half, chicken broth, ale, and Worcestershire. Simmer for 15 to 20 minutes, or until creamy and thick. Remove from heat. Stir in cheese, a handful at a time, until it's melted and smooth. Top each serving with Bacon Croutons.

Bacon Croutons: In a large skillet cook 4 slices bacon until crisp. Remove bacon from skillet and add 1½ cups 1-inch bread cubes, tossing bread cubes with bacon grease until coated. Cook and stir bread cubes over medium heat for 5 to 8 minutes or until nice and toasty. Meanwhile, chop cooked bacon slices and add to skillet during final minute of cooking.

butternut squash chili with lime sour cream

Makes about 6 servings.

2 tablespoons chili-flavored olive oil or
  olive oil

1 cup chopped onion

3 cloves garlic, minced

2 teaspoons chili powder

1 teaspoon hot smoked paprika *(or skip it*
  and use 3 teaspoons chili powder, total)

1 teaspoon ground cumin

3 cups peeled butternut squash chunks

1 28-ounce can diced tomatoes

2 19-ounce cans navy and/or pinto beans
  (rinsed and drained)

1 12-ounce can of beer, like Stella Artois *(or*
  whatever's in the fridge)

1 8-ounce can tomato sauce

1 cup water

⅓ teaspoon salt

Lime Sour Cream *(right)*

Optional toppings: shredded pepper Jack
  cheese, chopped fresh cilantro *(or even*
  corn chips like Fritos)

1. In a big soup pot, heat oil and cook onion, garlic, chili powder, paprika, and cumin over medium heat for 8 minutes or so, until onion is tender. Stir in the squash, undrained tomatoes, beans, beer, tomato sauce, water, and salt. Bring to boiling, then reduce heat. Simmer, covered, for 45 minutes to 1 hour.

2. Meanwhile, make Lime Sour Cream. Serve chili with a dollop of Lime Sour Cream. Pile on additional toppings of your choice.

Lime Sour Cream: Stir together ½ cup sour cream, ½ teaspoon shredded lime zest, 2 tablespoons fresh lime juice, and a dash of salt.

rum and cola super-crispy wings

Makes 8 to 10 appetizer servings.

3 pounds chicken wing drummettes

Salt and freshly ground black pepper

1 tablespoon chile-flavored olive oil

1 cup cola

¼ cup rum

3 to 4 tablespoons hot sauce

2 tablespoons honey

1 tablespoon butter

1. Preheat oven to 450°F. Line a 15x10x1-inch baking pan with foil. Add chile oil and chicken. Sprinkle with salt and pepper. Turn chicken in pan to coat with oil. Bake for 45 to 60 minutes or until chicken is deep golden brown and super crispy, carefully pouring off liquid at the halfway point (*seems like a long time at a high temp, but that's what makes them so awesome; just do it*).

2. While chicken bakes, in a small saucepan combine cola, rum, hot sauce, honey, and butter. Bring to boiling over high heat. Reduce heat to medium-low and simmer about 30 minutes or until it reduces to a thickened glaze.

3. Remove chicken from oven and brush generously with glaze; return to oven about 5 minutes more. Serve with remaining glaze and lots of napkins.

chimichurri stuffed pork chops

Makes 4 servings.

1 cup chopped fresh parsley

½ cup olive oil

¼ cup sauvignon blanc or other herbal
   white wine

2 tablespoons white wine vinegar

2 tablespoons fresh oregano

3 cloves garlic

1 small shallot, roughly chopped (*or a couple
   tablespoons of sweet onion*)

¼ teaspoon crushed red pepper

¼ teaspoon salt

¼ teaspoon pepper

4 pork chops, about 1½ inch thick

4 slices Manchego cheese (*or Monterey Jack*)

Cooked couscous or 1 quinoa

1. Preheat oven to 375°F. For chimichurri sauce, in a food processor combine all ingredients except pork chops and cheese. Pulse until chopped and combined. (*Don't get carried away and turn it into puree.*) Put half of the chimichurri sauce in a small bowl and set aside.

2. Make a pocket in each chop by cutting horizontally from one side almost to the opposite side. Sprinkle chops with salt and pepper. Put a slice of cheese in each pocket. Spoon remaining half of chimichurri sauce inside pockets and on outside of chops. Use toothpicks to hold pockets closed.

3. Put chops on a rack in a shallow roasting pan. Bake for 35 to 45 minutes or until juices run clear (*temperature should be 160°F*). Serve chops with cooked couscous or quinoa and the chimichurri sauce you set aside earlier. Don't eat the toothpicks.

tequila shrimp pasta

Makes 4 servings.

1 medium red sweet pepper, cut in strips

½ cup thin strips red onion

2 cloves garlic, minced

1 tablespoon olive oil

⅓ cup tequila

2 large tomatoes, chopped

1 chipotle in adobo sauce, chopped

1 tablespoon lime juice

¼ teaspoon salt

1 pound medium shrimp, peeled
    and deveined

12 ounces dried campanelle or gemelli pasta

2 green onions, chopped *(or chopped
    cilantro is good too)*

1. In a large skillet cook sweet pepper, onion, and garlic in hot oil over medium-high heat about 6 minutes or until tender and beginning to brown. Remove pan from heat. Carefully add tequila *(it can ignite, then where will you be?)*. Return to heat and simmer until tequila is cooked down by half. Add tomatoes, chipotle, lime juice, and salt. Cook until the tomatoes begin to break down and come to boiling. Add shrimp and cook, stirring, for 3 minutes, or until pink and opaque.

2. Meanwhile, cook the pasta according to package directions, except cook it for 1 to 2 minutes less than the time given on the package. Drain, reserving some of the pasta water.

3. Add the pasta to the sauce and cook, stirring, for 2 to 3 minutes, or until the mixture is creamy and pasta is tender. Add a little pasta water, if needed, to keep the sauce from getting too thick. Sprinkle with green onions.

double drunken dogs

Makes 8 servings.

2 12-ounce cans or bottles lager beer

1 small sweet onion, sliced

1 medium red sweet pepper, seeded, and cut in thin strips

8 all-beef hot dogs *(or 8 uncooked bratwursts)*

8 hot dog buns

Homemade Mustard with Ale *(page 120)*

Condiments of choice, such as pickle spears, relish, and shredded cheese)

1. In a big pot bring beer to boiling. Add onion and sweet pepper. Return to boiling. Reduce heat and simmer for 5 minutes. Prick hot dogs *(or brats)* several times with a fork. Add hot dogs to beer mixture and cook for 5 minutes more or until heated through. *(If using brats, simmer for 20 minutes more).* Fish out the hot dogs *(or brats).* Drain onion and sweet pepper.

2. Grill hot dogs over medium-hot coals for 3 to 5 minutes, turning frequently or until skins turn golden brown. Put the vegetables on a grill rack and cook alongside the dogs. They'll be ready at the same time. *(Brats will take a few minutes longer. But they're already cooked, so just eyeball 'em. They're ready when they look good.)* In fact, you can skip the grilling step altogether, but it adds additional smoky flavor.

3. Serve hot dogs on buns slathered with Homemade Mustard with Ale. Top dogs with grilled vegetables and condiments.

homemade mustard with ale

Makes ¾ cup mustard.

¼ cup yellow mustard seeds

⅓ cup pale ale

⅓ cup white wine vinegar

1 teaspoon olive oil

1 teaspoon brown sugar

¼ teaspoon salt

⅛ teaspoon turmeric

1. Combine all ingredients in a glass bowl or measuring cup. Cover and refrigerate overnight.

2. Transfer the mustard mixture to a food processor or blender *(the Magic Bullet is perfect for this)*, and whiz until it thickens to a mustardy consistency. Cover and store in the refrigerator for up to 2 weeks.

cardamom-spiced mandarin martini

1 cocktail, plus enough Cardamom Syrup to make a total of 6 cocktails.

Cardamom Syrup

½ cup sugar

½ cup water

1 teaspoon ground cardamom

¼ teaspoon ground cinnamon

The Martini

3 ounces mandarin vodka (*plain vodka works, but it's better with mandarin*)

1 ounce orange liqueur (*think Cointreau or Grand Marnier*)

1 ounce orange juice

2 teaspoons Cardamom Syrup

Halved kumquat or half-moon slice of orange

1. Make Cardamom Syrup by stirring together sugar, water, cardamom, and cinnamon in a pan over medium heat. Simmer for 10 minutes. Cool. Makes about 6 ounces.

2. To make one martini, fill a cocktail shaker with ice. Add mandarin vodka, orange liqueur, orange juice, and the 2 teaspoons Cardamom Syrup. Shake, shake, shake. Strain into a martini glass, and drop in the halved kumquat or orange slice.

berry gin and tonic

Makes 1 cocktail.

1 lime wedge

Fine sugar

1 ounce raspberry-flavored syrup

2 ounces gin

1 ounce *(a shot glass full)* **of blueberries**

3 to 4 raspberries

Tonic

1. Rub the lime wedge around the edge of a highball glass. Dip rim in fine sugar. Squeeze remaining juice from lime wedge into a glass. Fill glass with ice. Add raspberry syrup, gin, and berries. Top off with tonic. Serve with a spoon!

Gin and tonic is a classic with health benefits. It'll protect against malaria! *(Well, maybe not. But rumor has it that the cocktail was created by British soldiers who added gin to anti-malerial quinine to make the bitter tonic easier to take).*

tropical white wine sangria for a crowd

Makes 12 to 15 servings (more or less).

1 750-ml bottle dry white wine

1 750-ml bottle Moscato d'Asti* or
   white wine

1 liter bottle club soda, chilled *(Lindsey skips*
   the club soda when she makes this)

2 cups fresh pineapple chunks

1 cup cubed papaya or mango

1 lime, sliced

1. Pour wine and club soda in a pitcher. Add fruit and stir gently. Serve over ice. Be sure to scoop some of the fruit into each glass. *(If you want to make this in advance, stir the pineapple and papaya chunks into the dry white wine and refrigerate up to 8 hours. Add the Moscato d'Asti, club soda, and lime slices just before serving.)*

*Moscato d'Asti is a low-alcohol wine that tastes like summer. It is subtly sweet with a hint of fizz—about half the effervescence of most sparkling wines.

Michelle Medley, Dallas, Texas

creating my own leap year

Sitting cross-legged, I was flipping magazine pages in a doctor's waiting room when these words jumped out at me: "What are you waiting for?"

I read on. "Our deepest fear is not that we're inadequate. Our deepest fear is that we are powerful beyond all measure. It is our light, not our darkness, that most frightens us. We ask ourselves, 'Who am I to be brilliant, gorgeous, talented, and fabulous?' Actually, who are you not to be? You are a child of God. Your playing small does not serve the world," said the article, quoting from Marianne Williamson's book, *A Return to Love.*

Even the most confident of us will give away the power we have to step forward and change things. We give it up all the time. Two more phrases made me tear out the article and stuff it in my bag.

1. FEAR is nothing more or less than False Evidence Appearing Real.
2. The greatest trapeze flyers are also the greatest fallers. They don't think of falling as failing. They think of it as part of their aerial acrobatics.

And that got me pondering: "What if the thing you fear doing or changing is nothing more than false evidence appearing real? If you could take the fear of failure—or falling—out of the equation, what could you do with your power?" Soon after, I got the answer.

Out of the blue, a woman I barely knew invited me to spend the remaining days of summer working in her bakery. Her location: a small town in Wyoming.

Bread and I have had an indecent romance for years, and I wanted the chance to explore that ardent love more fully. I was afraid to take time off from my cubicle job, fearful that the company would eliminate it while I was gone. Scared to pieces, I threw my heart over the bar, just like a trapeze artist, and leaped. Heading west along with me was my mother's ukulele, a copy of *Like Water for Chocolate*, a pair of tap shoes, flowers made into Frida Kahlo headpieces, CDs of Pink Martini and Fats Waller, and a vintage black kimono. And I picked up a bottle of citrus-flavored Patron when I arrived. I felt prepared for anything.

I wanted to throw my heart open, curl my fingers around a handful of dough, and roll it into perfectly shaped roll after roll and place them in Zenlike rows on baking sheets. I wanted to deliver those rolls to the back door of the Cowboy Café—like a bootlegging bread maker. I wanted to see, smell, touch, and taste everything in a place not my own.

My goal was to make daily bread for the town, but I ended up baking bread for the funeral of one of the town's most respected elders—my host's own father. I didn't plan on feeling heartbreak, fresh and overflowing, but it found me. Yet I recovered, as we always do. And I began leaping with wild abandon, embracing my indecent romance with dough and tasting life's boldest flavors. After all, what am I waiting for?

At 54, Michelle Medley took another big leap, enrolling in the baking and pastry program at Le Cordon Bleu in Dallas, where heartbreak can usually be fixed with good knives and more butter.

happy endings

Eat chocolate, feel sexy.
Just ask Casanova, who reportedly
downed a cup of hot chocolate
before each amorous adventure.
Bite into any sweet treat and you'll
quickly go from cranky to calm.

mexican chocolate glazed grapes

Makes about 6 dessert or snack servings.

½ pound seedless grapes, broken into little clusters of 2 to 3 grapes

4 ounces bittersweet and/or semisweet chocolate, coarsely chopped

½ teaspoon agave nectar or honey

¼ to ½ teaspoon cinnamon

Finely chopped nuts *(whatever you've got)*

1. Wash and dry grapes thoroughly. *(Even a few drops of water will ruin melted chocolate.)*

2. Combine chocolate, agave nectar, and cinnamon in a small pan. Cook over low heat until chocolate is melted. *(Or heat in a microwave-safe bowl in the microwave oven, stirring every minute or so until melted.)*

3. Remove from heat and dip small bunches of grapes into chocolate *(don't worry about covering entire grapes)*. Dip into nuts, place on a wax-paper-lined cookie sheet, and cool until chocolate is set. *(Or pop the cookie sheet into the fridge or freezer until cooled. In fact, once they're frozen, transfer the little bunches to a plastic freezer bag and keep them in the freezer for up to 3 months. Nibble at will.)*

dark and dreamy

Chocolate really should come with a medical seal of approval.

Anyone who has ever reached for dark chocolate while in the throes of disaster, depression, or deadline pressure knows all about the feel-good endorphins stimulated by chocolate.

There's so more to chocolate than meets the taste buds.

• **Energy flagging at work?** Suck on a bit of chocolate. The caffeine in chocolate can act as a quick pick-me-up.

• **Dark chocolate,** with a cacao content of 65% or more is best for your health.

• **Antioxidants in dark chocolate** are good for your heart. A daily nibble of dark chocolate has been shown to reduce blood pressure and LDL (bad) cholesterol. Raw, organic dark chocolate contains the most antioxidants.

• **Dark chocolate's antioxidant** content may protect your skin from sun damage, according to studies.

• **The serotonin** in chocolate may serve as an anti-depressant.

• **Chocolate simply tastes good.**

double chocolate stout cupcakes

Makes 12 cupcakes.

1 cup all-purpose flour

½ teaspoon baking soda

¼ teaspoon salt

½ cup chocolate stout *(pour about ⅓ cup chocolate stout plus foam, let settle for 1 to 2 minutes, scoop off the foam, and you should have about ½ cup)*

½ cup butter *(unsalted, please; if you're using salted butter, ditch the salt above)*

⅓ cup unsweetened cocoa powder

3 ounces dark unsweetened chocolate, coarsely chopped, or semisweet dark chocolate chips

¾ cup packed brown sugar

2 slightly beaten eggs

Dark Chocolate Frosting *(next page)*

Coarse sea salt

12 bite-size pretzels

1. Preheat oven to 350°F. Line muffin pan with 12 paper liners. Set aside. Stir together flour, soda, and salt. Set aside.

2. In a medium saucepan over medium heat and stirring frequently, bring stout, butter, and cocoa just to simmer. Add dark chocolate, stirring until melted. Remove from heat. Add brown sugar, stirring until smooth. Whisk in eggs until combined. Add flour mixture, beating until smooth.

3. Fill cupcake liners about three-fourths full. Bake for about 15 minutes or until toothpick inserted in center comes out clean. *(Or just tap the top of the cupcake with your finger. It should bounce back.)* Cool in pan on rack for 5 minutes, then carefully remove cupcakes from muffin pan and cool completely on rack.

4. Frost with Dark Chocolate Frosting recipe. Sprinkle coarse salt over each cupcake. Top with a pretzel.

dark chocolate frosting

Makes enough to cover 12 cupcakes.

¼ cup unsalted butter

¼ cup milk *(or cream as long as we're being decadent)*

1 cup dark chocolate chips *(or 8 ounces dark chocolate, coarsely chopped)*

2½ cups sifted powdered sugar

1. In a small saucepan, heat the butter and milk over medium heat until butter is melted and mixture is bubbly, stirring constantly. Reduce heat to low and stir in dark chocolate until melted.

2. Remove pan from heat and add powdered sugar. Beat by hand until smooth. Cool to room temperature. Stir well before frosting cupcakes.

CHOCOLATE CHEER
Dark chocolate not only tastes good, but delivers a mighty dose of antioxidants that have been found to lower blood pressure. Perhaps a brownie a day will chase your worries away?

walnut-studded dark chocolate brownies

Makes 16 brownies.

½ cup butter

4 ounces bittersweet chocolate *(70% cacao)*, coarsely chopped

½ cup granulated sugar

½ cup dark brown sugar

2 eggs

½ cup all-purpose flour

½ teaspoon baking powder

1½ cups coarsely chopped walnuts, toasted

½ cup milk chocolate or semisweet chocolate pieces

1. Preheat oven to 350°F. Line an 8x8x2-inch or 9x9x2-inch baking pan with foil, leaving an overhang on opposite sides. *(You'll thank us for this later when you don't have to clean the pan.)*

2. In a medium saucepan, combine butter and bittersweet chocolate. Cook and stir over medium heat until butter and chocolate are melted. Remove from heat. Using a wooden spoon, stir granulated sugar and brown sugar into chocolate mixture until smooth. Add eggs, beating with spoon until well combined.

3. In a small bowl, combine flour and baking powder. Stir flour mixture into the chocolate mixture just until combined. Stir in nuts and milk chocolate pieces *(batter will be thick).* Spread in prepared pan. Bake for 25 minutes or until top is set but still soft. *(Skip the toothpick test because the center is going to be gooey.)* Cool on a wire rack. Carefully lift out the foil along with the slab of brownies. Remove foil and cut brownies into into bars.

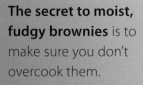

The secret to moist, fudgy brownies is to make sure you don't overcook them.

coconut rum crispy treats

Makes about 12 servings.

3 tablespoons butter

**1 10-ounce package regular marshmallows
    or 4 cups mini marshmallows**

6 cups Kellogg's Rice Krispies cereal

3 cups coconut, toasted _(or not toasted)_

1 cup dark chocolate chips

2 tablespoons butter

½ cup powdered sugar

**2 tablespoons coconut rum or spiced rum _(or
    milk if you're sharing with the kiddies)_**

1. Line a 13x9-inch pan with foil or parchment paper with an overhang on both ends _(or the long sides; you need enough foil to grasp when you want to lift the treats from the pan later)._ Butter the foil. Nonstick cooking spray works too.

2. Melt butter in a large pan over medium-low heat. Add marshmallows; stir until melted. Remove from heat. Stir. Add cereal and 2 cups of the coconut, stirring and stirring until everything is combined. Spoon mixture into pan. If you left enough of an overhang you can just fold the foil over the top of the treats and pat nicely until all is even so you don't have to get your hands sticky.

3. Melt the chocolate and butter in a small pan over very, very, very low heat or in the microwave oven. _(Put the chocolate and butter in a micro-safe bowl and cook for 1 minute on 70% power. Stir. If not melted, cook for 10 seconds and stir again. Continue at 10-second intervals until it's all melted.)_ Stir in powdered sugar and rum. Spread over treats. Sprinkle with remaining toasted coconut. Cut into squares and have at it.

peach-blueberry slab pie

Makes 15 to 25 slabs *(depending on how you cut 'em).*

3 ¼ cups flour

1 tsp. salt

½ cup shortening

½ cup butter

1 egg yolk

Milk

4 to 5 cups sliced peaches

2 to 3 cups blueberries, fresh or frozen *(if frozen, don't thaw)*

¾ cup sugar

3 tablespoons cornstarch

1 teaspoon ground cinnamon

1 recipe Vanilla Glaze *(below)*

1. For pastry, in a large bowl, stir together flour and salt. Use a pastry blender to cut in shortening and butter until mixture resembles small peas. Lightly beat egg yolk in a glass measuring cup. Add enough milk to the egg yolk to make ¾ cup; mix well. Mix egg yolk mixture into flour mixture until it holds together. Divide dough into two-thirds and one-third portions. (If you wrap and chill dough at this point, it's easier to work with. If you're in a hurry, it's OK to keep going.)

2. Roll out larger portion of dough on a floured surface into an 18x12-inch rectangle. Carefully transfer it into a 15x10x1-inch baking pan. (I roll pastry around rolling pin and then unroll over baking pan.)

3. Preheat oven to 375°F. For filling, combine peaches, blueberries, sugar, cornstarch, and cinnamon. Toss to coat. Spread evenly into crust.

4. Roll remaining dough into a 16x11-inch rectangle. Place over fruit. Bring bottom pastry up and over top pastry. Seal edges with tines of fork. Prick top of pastry surface all over with fork.

5. Bake for 40 to 50 minutes or until light brown. Cool. Drizzle with Vanilla Glaze.

Vanilla Glaze: In a small bowl stir together 1½ cups sifted powdered sugar, 1 teaspoon vanilla, and enough milk (4 to 5 teaspoons) to make a thick glaze.

mom's apple pie with crumbly topping

Makes 8 servings.

1¼ cups all-purpose flour

¼ teaspoon salt

⅓ cup shortening

1 teaspoon vinegar

4 to 5 tablespoons ice water

¼ cup granulated sugar

2 tablespoons all-purpose flour

½ teaspoon ground cinnamon

⅛ teaspoon salt

**6 cups thinly sliced, peeled tart cooking apples
(about 2¼ pounds)**

¾ cup packed brown sugar

½ cup all-purpose flour

½ teaspoon ground cinnamon

⅓ cup butter

1 cup chopped walnuts

1. In a medium mixing bowl stir together 1¼ cups flour and ¼ teaspoon salt. Using a pastry blender, cut in shortening until pieces are pea-size. Sprinkle with vinegar and 1 tablespoon of the water; gently toss with a fork. Add 1 tablespoon of water at a time, tossing with fork, until all dough is moistened. Form into a ball.

2. Roll dough into a 12-inch circle. Transfer to a 9-inch pie plate. Trim pastry to ½ inch beyond edge of pie plate. Fold extra pastry under. Press the tines of a fork around edge. Set aside.

3. Preheat oven to 375°F. In a large bowl stir together sugar, 2 tablespoons flour, ½ teaspoon cinnamon, and ⅛ teaspoon salt. Add apple slices. Gently toss to combine. Spoon apple mixture on pastry.

4. For topping, stir together brown sugar, ½ cup flour, and ½ teaspoon cinnamon. Using a pastry blender, cut in butter until everything looks crumbly. Stir in walnuts. Sprinkle crumb mixture over apple mixture. Gently pat down.

5. Place pie on a baking sheet. Cover entire pie loosely with foil. Bake for 15 minutes. Remove foil. Bake for 35 to 40 minutes more or until top is dark golden brown and apples are tender. Cool on a wire rack.

chocolate cake with peanut butter frosting

Makes 10 to 12 servings.

1 cup flour

½ cup unsweetened cocoa powder

½ teaspoon baking soda

¼ teaspoon baking powder

¼ teaspoon salt

6 tablespoons butter, softened

1 cup sugar

1 egg, at room temperature (a cold egg keeps your cake from rising as tall as it should)

1 teaspoon vanilla

¾ cup buttermilk (milk also works)

2 ounces dark chocolate, chopped (substitute semisweet chips if you aren't feeling bitter)

Peanut Butter Frosting (next page)

Bittersweet Chocolate Glaze (next page)

Peanuts

1. Preheat oven to 350° F. Grease and lightly flour an 8- or 9-inch round baking pan.

2. Stir together flour, cocoa, baking soda, baking powder, and salt. Then move it out of your way while you put the butter in a big bowl and beat it with a mixer until it's creamy *(30 seconds, give or take)*. Add sugar a bit at a time, continuing to beat *(medium speed, please)* until it's light and fluffy. Beat in egg and vanilla. Alternately add flour mixture, then buttermilk, beating on low speed after each addition until combined. *(Don't overmix.)* With a spoon, stir in bittersweet chocolate. Pour into pan. It's kinda thick so spread evenly with a rubber spatula.

3. Bake for 35 to 40 minutes for an 8-inch pan, or 30 to 35 minutes for a 9-inch pan, or until a toothpick comes out clean. Cool on a wire rack for 10 minutes. Remove cake from pan. Cool completely on a wire rack.

4. Frost with Peanut Butter Frosting. Chill in the fridge for 15 minutes or so. Slowly pour Chocolate Glaze over top of cake. Sprinkle peanuts in the center *(or all over the top; go nuts, heehee)*.

peanut butter frosting

1 ½ cups powdered sugar

¾ cup creamy peanut butter *(don't use natural because you don't want the oil separating)*

¼ cup butter, softened

1 teaspoon vanilla extract

2 to 4 tablespoons milk

1. Beat together powdered sugar, peanut butter, butter, and vanilla until smooth. Add milk, if needed to make it easy to spread.

dark chocolate glaze

3 ounces dark chocolate, chopped *(⅔ cup)*

3 tablespoons butter, cut into small pieces

1 teaspoon light corn syrup

1. Melt chocolate and butter in a small pan over low heat, stirring contantly. Stir in corn syrup; cool slightly.

caramelized cardamom peaches and ice cream

Makes 2 servings.

2 tablespoons unsalted butter

1 peach, pitted and cut into 8 wedges

1 tablespoon coconut rum or spiced rum

¼ teaspoon ground cardamom

⅛ teaspoon cinnamon

2 tablespoons packed light brown sugar

Ice cream

1 tablespoon coarsely chopped

pecans, toasted

1. Heat butter in a skillet over medium heat. Add peach slices, rum, cardamom, and cinnamon. Cook for 3 to 4 minutes, or until sauce begins to thicken, turning peaches occasionally. Add brown sugar and cook for 1 to 2 minutes more. Let cool slightly.

2. Serve peaches and sauce over ice cream. Top with pecans.

**SPICE UP
YOUR LOVE LIFE**
The intoxicating allure of cardamom permeates some of the tales in *One Thousand and One Nights* (also known as *Arabian Nights*) where the spice is used to make love potions. Cookbook author and writer Monica Bhide has experienced its fragrant and romantic power in a big way. See *"Love in the Time of Cardamom"* (next page).

Monica Bhide, Washington D.C.

love in the time of cardamom

I was a lonely graduate student in an unfamiliar land. The year was 1991, and I had just moved to the United States—Lynchburg, Virginia, to be exact. It was a tiny town, and I felt very alone. Coming from India, a country of a billion people, to a city of a few thousand was a huge adjustment.

At holiday time, most of the students had gone home. In between wishing I could go back to visit my family and crying myself to sleep, I decided to cook. If I couldn't go to my mother, I would bring her to me! I borrowed ingredients from neighbors and friends and began preparing my mother's rice pudding. The crushed cardamom that adorned the pudding spread its aroma, perfuming the air in and around the house.

In the midst of my cooking, there came a knock on my apartment door. "I just had to find out where the aroma of 'home' was coming from," said a handsome, young Indian graduate student. I had seen him before at the library but had not met him. We started chatting about home as the enticing perfume of cardamom created a connection between two homesick strangers.

That young grad student, now my husband, has been enamored of my cooking ever since.

P.S. We have two amazing boys, and they love hearing the story of how we met as much as they love cardamom!

Monica Bhide, is an engineer turned food writer and cookbook author. Her recipe for Rice Pudding and Mango Parfait can be found in her book Modern Spice (Simon & Schuster 2009).

index

mexican chocolate glazed grapes, 130
mom's apple pie with crumbly topping, 137
over the moon chocolate chip cookies, 78
peach-blueberry slab pie, 136
walnut-studded dark chocolate brownies, 134

PASTA/RICE
build your own sushi, 57
fried rice with portuguese sausage, 32
lemon chicken lasagna, 41
mushroom smothered chicken with pasta, 66
obnoxiously cheesy and easy mac 'n' cheese, 70
over-the-rainbow chard pasta, 84
tequila shrimp pasta, 120
very lemon pasta with spinach, 42

POULTRY
deli chicken with blue cheese dunking sauce, 97
easy lemon garlic chicken, 40
seriously easy roast chicken, 72
thai lettuce chicken wraps, 53

SALADS/SIDES/VEGETARIAN
crunchy apple salad, 95
feta potato salad, 96
garlic mashed potatoes, 75
it's-greek-to-me salad, 82
kick-ass guajillo sauced enchiladas, 76
lemony chickpea and herb salad, 43
mexican street corn, 88
outrageous marinated veggie kabobs, 110

poblano pepper slaw with orange dressing, 85
roasted asparagus and carrots with lemon oil, 44
total satisfaction salad, 87
watermelon salad with cotija cheese, 94

SEAFOOD
asian shrimp noodles with vegetables, 59
furikake-crusted tuna steaks, 109
green curry shrimp and green beans, 58
spicy crab salad, 56
super-fast shrimp, spinach, and bow-ties, 86
tropical salmon salad with mango and avocado, 108
white bean tuna salad, 98

SOUPS/STEWS/CHILI
ale-cheddar soup with bacon croutons, 116
beef barley stew, 68
butternut squash chili with lime sour cream, 117
fresh chunky tomato soup with pesto, 69
tom kha gai soup, 54

about the authors

Jeanne Ambrose and Lindsey Ambrose are a mother-daughter seasoned food-writing team.

Jeanne is a contributing writer/editor for *Better Homes and Gardens, Organic Gardening, Healthy Cooking, Diabetic Living,* and other magazines.

Lindsey, also a writer, has been a foodie since she was old enough to grasp a wooden spoon and lick off the batter. She has cooked for Food Not Bombs in San Francisco and eaten her way through Italy, Mexico, and Hawaii, where she was born.

For more on **Heartbreak Recovery Kitchen**™, including information on ordering books, visit

heartbreakrecoverykitchen.com